INFORMATION & COMMUNICATION TECHNOLOGY SYSTEM MAINTENANCE FIRST YEAR ICTSM

OBJECTIVE QUESTION ANSWERS

MANOJ DOLE

Digitization is the need of the time. In the future, training in industrial training institutes will need to be conducted using online internet to make training more convenient and easy. E-books containing a set of MCQ questions will be made available to the trainees as they need to be more accustomed to the multiple choice questions MCQ to prepare for the online exams taking place in their industrial training institutes.

With all these factors in mind, Mr. Manoj Madhukar Dole Instructor, Industrial Training Institute, Satara, has written books according to the new annual system and NSQF-5 syllabus. And they've created theoretical mobile apps and blogs to make training easier, and made all these educational materials available for download on the world famous websites Google Play Store, Amazon and Apple Book Store.

The books were published by Hon'ble Joint Director Shri Rajendra Ghume Saheb Regional Office of Vocational Education and Training, Pune on 9/1/2019, at this time Shri Prakash Saigavkar Saheb Principal Government Industrial Training Institute Aundh Pune, Shri Tukaram Misal Saheb Principal Govt. Q. Sanstha Satara, Shri Sachin Dhumal Saheb District Vocational Education and Training Officer Satara, Shri Yatin Pargaonkar Saheb Principal Govt. Q. Sanstha Kolhapur, Shri Vikas Teke Saheb Inspector Vocational Education and Training Regional Office Pune, Palekar Foods Products Pvt. Ltd. Entrepreneurial Chairman of Satara Mr. Nilkanthrao Palekar Saheb, Chairman of Hira Foods Mr. Ibrahim Baba Tamboli Saheb, Mrs. Shalmali Pawar Headmaster Government Technical School Center Satara and other dignitaries were present on the occasion.

Contents

Prologue

Information & Communication Technology System Maintenance First Year ICTSM is a simple Book for ITI & Engineering Course Information & Communication Technology System Maintenance ICTSM. It contains objective questions with underlined & bold correct answers MCQ covering all topics including all about the latest & Important about safety and environment, use of fire extinguishers, Resistors and Soldering, De-soldering practice,Inductors, measure Inductance and uses of Transformer, Capacitor, types of Transistors and use it as Amplifiers, voltage, frequency, modulation of modulator/ transmitter. Working with some important Mechanical, Electrical & Electronics Accessories used in information communication system, Word Processing and Spreadsheet Software, hardware components of Desktop Computer., Operating System and all other application software, hardware components of Laptop PC. Replace/ install SMPS and troubleshoot, memory devices, chips, Modem, System Resources, Add on Cards, Cables & Connectors, Tablet/ Smart Devices, Networking System using various network devices, configuration of Windows Server. Installation, configuration of DNS, Routing and user account customization. Configuration of Server and managing Server Network security and Infrastructure. Installation and basic configuration of Linux server and lots more.

We add new question answers with each new version. Please email us in case of any errors/omissions. This is arguably the largest and best Book for All engineering multiple choice questions and answers.

As a student you can use it for your exam prep. This Book is also useful for professors to refresh material.

Foreword

Vocational education and training is imparted through the Department of Vocational Education and Training through the Department of Business Education and Business Practical to supply multi-skilled artisans in line with the rapidly growing demand in the industrial sector in the 21st century. All the occupations within the institutions are important, as the trainees from these occupations develop multi-skills as per the demands of the industry.

with the noble intention of making available MCQ e-books suitable for all businesses, considering that all the examinations in all the industries in the industrial sector are conducted online and include MCQ method questions. Mr. Manoj Madhukar Dole has written a very good e-book on MCQ method as per the new annual syllabus. This e-book will definitely be a guide for all the trainees, trainee candidates, training instructors and others concerned.

The author of the book is Mr. Manoj Madhukar Dole, Instructor Gov. ITI Satara has 17 years of training experience. Written as a new annual pattern, this e-book incorporates modern digital QR Code technology to understand the layout, simple language, and simple syntax, diagrams and videos for each subject. So I am sure that this e-book will definitely be useful for in-depth study and exam practice. The work they have done is certainly commendable.

Mr. Tukaram Misal
Principal Government Industrial Training Institute Satara.

Preface

DGET New Delhi and CSTARI Kolkata have been implementing an annual pattern for all businesses in ITI since the August 2018 session. The examination system will also be changed and it will be online from this year and since all the questions are of Objective Type (MCQ), the trainees are in dire need of in-depth study. It is with this in mind that we are delighted to present the books based on the old NIMI pattern and a complete overview of the new annual pattern, and we hope that these books will be a guide for all business directors and trainees. Is.

For writing these books, Johar Awate Saheb, Principal of ITI Akluj. Former Principal of ITI Satara Saigavkar Saheb, Assistant Director Shri Chandrakant Dhekne Saheb Regional Office of Vocational Education and Training, Pune, District Vocational Education and Training Officer Sachin Dhumal Saheb and Headmaster Government Technical School Kendra Shalmali Pawar Madam and son Adhiraj Dole, mother Kusum Dole, I am very grateful to my father Madhukar Dole and wife Ashwini Dole for their special guidance and cooperation from time to time.

Also, in a very short period of time, the book was reviewed by Shri Rajendra Ghume Saheb, Joint Director, Vocational Education and Training Regional Office, Pune, for his invaluable time in publishing the book. I am sincerely grateful for their feedback.

I am grateful to the Instructor of ITI Satara for there continuous support from the very beginning of writing the book.

From this book, I consider myself blessed to have shared my thoughts on e-learning with you. I will not claim that this book is perfect, because considering the perfection, this book is an attempt and is in its infancy. They will be valuable for improvement if they are tested and suggested.

Manoj Dole
Dated 9/1/2019

Acknowledgements

The industrial training and theoretical examination system of our industrial training institutes and these changes have been accepted by the craft instructors and the trainees. Theoretical examinations conducted in your industrial training institutes are also conducted online. Since these examinations are of multiple choice MCQ method, the trainees will need to get more practice of such questions.

With all these considerations in mind, Mr. Manoj Madhukar, Director, Dole Crafts, Katari Industrial Training Institute, Satara, has done a thorough study and with his diligent work and added his keen intellect, according to the new annual system and NSQF-5 syllabus, e-book of Katari and other machine trades. -Book) and they have created mobile apps and blogs on theoretical topics to make training easier and have made all these educational materials available for download on the world famous websites Google Play Store, Amazon and Apple Book Store. Training has been made easier by creating a print version and using advanced techniques like QR Code.

All these educational materials will definitely be a guide for all the trainees for in-depth study and for the craft instructors and other concerned who are imparting vocational training.

CHAPTER ONE

ICTSM First Year Drawings

ITI Book MCQ - Manoj Dole

www.itibook.com

www.itigov.blogspot.com   www.jobapprentices.blogspot.com   www.ititests.blogspot.com

www.itibook.com

www.itibook.com

megger
motor
multimeter
ohmmeter
resistores
star connected
alternator
voltmeter
ammeter
wattmeter

www.itibook.com 

COMPUTER PARTS

www.itigov.blogspot.com   www.jobapprentices.blogspot.com   www.ititests.blogspot.com

www.itibook.com

www.itibook.com

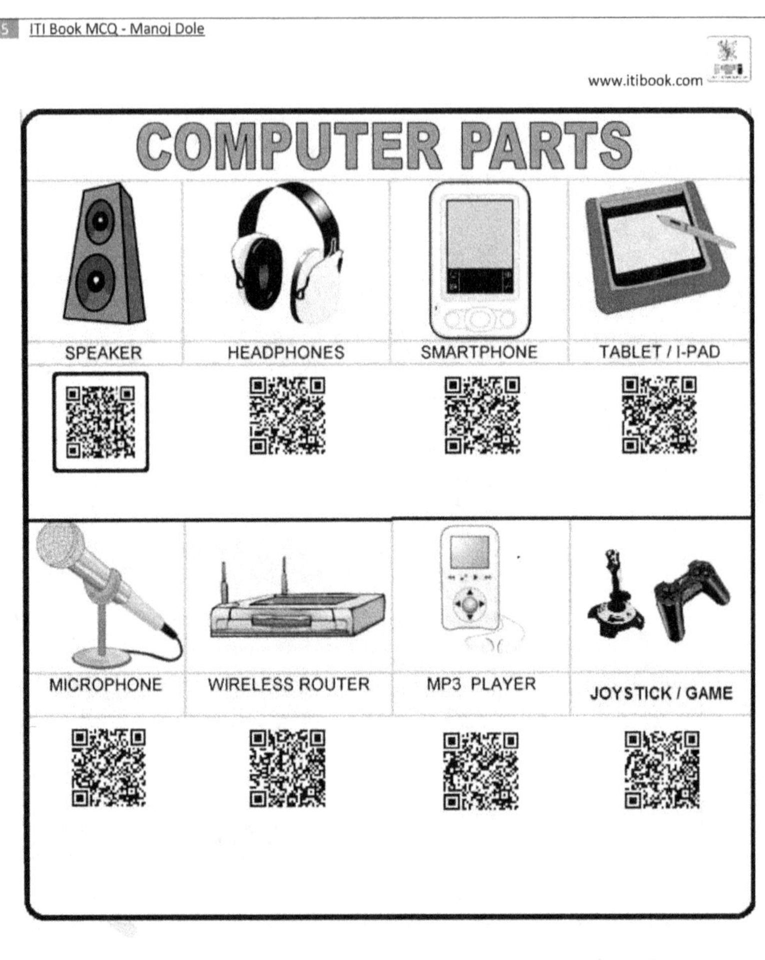

www.itibook.com

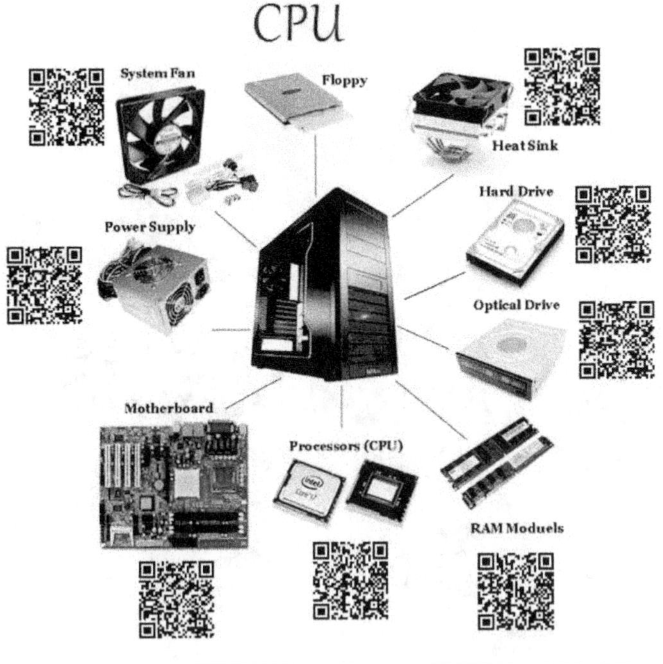

Computer CPU
Hardware Components

www.itigov.blogspot.com   www.jobapprentices.blogspot.com   www.ititests.blogspot.com

www.itibook.com

Matheeboad
Heatsink and Fan
Memory
Power Supply
CPU
Vodeo Card
Dvd Burner
Motherboard
Hard Drive
Motherboard
Hardware Components

www.itibook.com

Excel Basic Functions

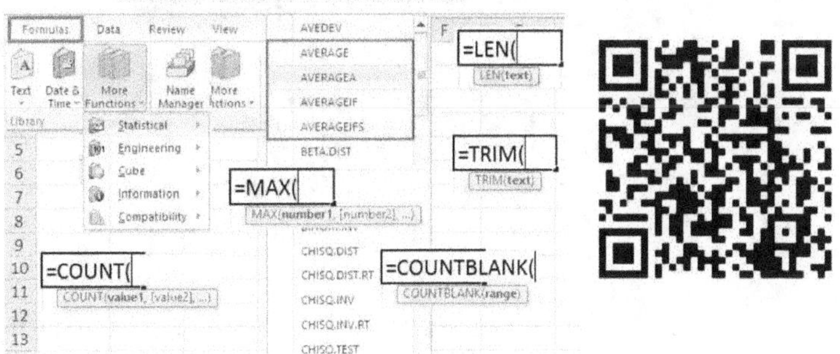

www.itibook.com

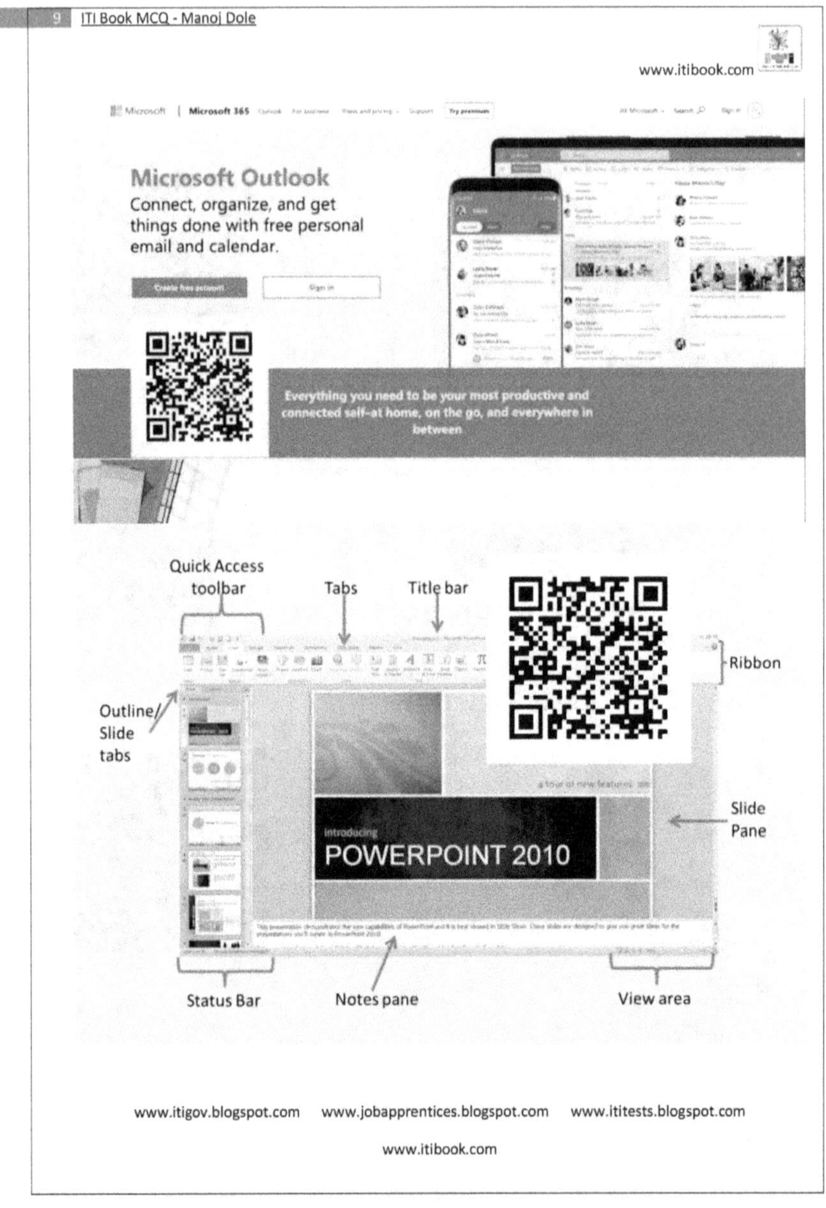

www.itibook.com

www.itibook.com

www.itigov.blogspot.com   www.jobapprentices.blogspot.com   www.ititests.blogspot.com

www.itibook.com

Enter Caption

CHAPTER TWO

ICTSM First Year MCQ

1] ABC stands for --------------
   A] Automatic Breathing Control
   B] Automatic Blood Control
   C] Airway Breathing Circulation
   D] Automatic Blood Circulation

Fire extinguisher

3] To put off"Class B" fire, the types of fire extinguisher used is ....
A] dry power
B] Carbon dioxide
C] Jet of water
D] Foam type
4] Which type of fire extinguisher is used to put off general fire?
A] Water type Extinguisher
B] Foam type Extinguisher
C] Dry chemical powder Extinguisher
D] Carbon dioxide (C02] Extinguisher
5] In case of bleeding, take treatment Of
D] cold 3" and rest
A] spray cold water
B] Bandage immediately -----.

B] Enquire about the accident thought treatment

6] in case of an accident, the victim should im
A] Asked to take rest
C] Attended immediately
D] leave him

7] First aid is given to an injured or ill person primarily....
A] Save life
B] Prevent further deterioration of the muff's
C] Give best possible comfort
D] All of these

84] Which one of the following fire extinguisher is suitable for a live electrical fire?
A] halon
B] water
C] foam
D] liquefied chemical

85] A heater draws a current of 8A when connected to a 240V source] What is the resistance value of the heater element in ohms?
A] 40
B] 20
C] 30
D] 60

86] An electric soldering iron with an 80 ohms heating element is plugged into a 240V outlet] How much current will be drawn by the iron?
A] 2A
B] 3A
C] 4A
D] 5A

87] The alternator in a car delivers 4A and has a load of 3 ohms connected across its terminals] Find the voltage of the circuit
A] 18V

B] 24V

C] 12V

D] 16V

88] Three resistors of 1K ohms, 2K ohms and 7K ohms are connected in series with a 30 V supply] If 2 K ohms and 7 K ohms resistors are open circuited, a voltmeter connected across the 7K ohms resistor will indicate...

A] 10 k ohms, 3A

B] 10 k ohms, 300mA

C] 10 k ohms, 3 mA

D] 5 k ohms, 6 mA

89] A voltage source produces an IR drop of 40V across a 20 ohms resistance, 60V across a 30 ohms resistance and 180V across a 90 ohms resistance all in series] How much is the applied voltage?

A] 180 V

B] 240 V

C] 100 V

D] 280 V

90] Three resistors 27 ohms, 47 ohms and 68 ohms are connected in parallel] What is the otal resistance?

A] less than 27 ohms

B] greater than 68 ohms

C] between 27 and 47 ohms

D] sum of all the three resistances

91] One million and one mege ohms resistors are there if connected both in parallel, what would be the combined resistance value?

A] 0.5 mega ohm

B] 0.5 milli ohm

C] 0.5 kilo ohm

D] 0.5 ohm

92] A 24 ohms and a 8 ohms resistors in parallel gets a combined resistance of...

A] 6 ohms

B] 12 ohms

C] 3 ohms

D] 32 ohms

93] Resistors of the following values are connected in parallel, 5 ohms, 5 kilo-ohms, 50 kilo-ohms, 5 mega ohms] Their equivalent resistance will be very near to...

A] <u>4.5 ohms</u>
B] 4500 ohms
C] 45000 ohms
D] 4,500,000 ohms

94] The resistance of given wire is 2 ohms] The resistance of the other wire made of the same material having twice the length and twice the cross sectional area is...
A] 5 ohms
B] 6 ohms
C] <u>2 ohms</u>
D] 8 ohms

95] If the area of a metal wire of a given length is doubles, its resistance will...
A] be doubled
B] <u>be halved</u>
C] remain the same
D] be four times more

96].Among the following only one is regarded as resistance wire
A] gold
B] silver
C] <u>nichrome</u>
D] copper

97] Arc heating occurs when the air between electrodes of opposite polarity becomes..
A] moistened
B] dry
C] <u>ionized</u>
D] none of the above

98] The meter used to measure the temperature of furnace is...
A] hydrometer
B] <u>pyrometer</u>
C] hygrometer
D] tachometer

99] in the case of electrolyte a rise in temperature causes...
A] <u>decrease in resistance</u>
B] increase in resistance
C] no change in resistance
D] none of the above

100] Heat developed in a conductor is proportional to the...
A] square of the power
B] square of the resistance
C] <u>square of the current</u>
D] square of the time
101] Out of the four metal/alloys given below, one has almost no change in resistance for temperature change...
A] nickel
B] nichrome
C] platinum
D] <u>manganin</u>
102] A material that is slightly repelled by a magnet is called ...
A] magnetic
B] paramagnetic
C] <u>diamagnetic</u>
D] ferromagnetic
103] A material that can be magnetized only very slightly is called...
A] magnetic
B] <u>paramagnetic</u>
C] diamagnetic
D] ferromagnetic
104] Substances that can be magnetized easily and make very strong magnets are called...
A] <u>ferromagnetic</u>
B] diamagnetic
C] paramagnetic
D] permanent magnetic
105] A substance that has a high retentivity can be used for the manufacture of...
A] electromagnets
B] <u>permanent magnets</u>
C] temporary magnets
D] paramagnets
106] A substance that has low retentivity can be used for the manufacture of...
A] <u>electromagnets</u>
B] permanent magnets
C] bar magnets

D] paramagnets

107] The symbol for inductance is...

A] H

B] I

C] L

D] X

108] Tube lamp choke is the best example of...

A] open circuited

B] short circuited

C] grounded

D] connected to the neutral line

109] The initial function of a choke in a tube light circuit is to...

A] limit the starting current

B] induce high voltage

C] heat up the filament

D] limit the current after starting

110] The second function of a choke in a tube light circuit is to...

A] limit the starting current

B] induce high voltage

C] heat up the filament

D] limit the current after starting

111] The periodic time of a wave from is 2ms] Calculate the frequency

A] 50 HZ

B] 5 HZ

C] 500HZ

D] 5 KHZ

112] How big is the peak amplitude of a sine-wave with an effective
value of 220 volts?

A] 311 V

B] 380 V

C] 400 V

D] 440 V

113] The peak-to-peak voltage is 99V] how big is the effective value of
the sine wave?

A] 70 V

B] 44.5V

C] 49.5 V

D] 35 V

114] A moving coil voltmeter reads 10 V AC] How big is the effective voltage?

A] higher

B] lower

C] <u>the same</u>

D] 10% higher

115] A moving iron ammeter reads 10 A] how big is the peak current of the oscillation?

A] 7.07 A

B] 1.1414A

C] 70.7 A

D] <u>14.1 A</u>

116] A current of 2 amps flows through a resistance of 10 ohms] The power dissipated in the resistance is equal to...

A] 20 watts

B] 200 watts

C] <u>40 watts</u>

D] 5 watts

117] If the frequency changes from 50 HZ to 100 HZ keeping voltage constant, the inductive reactance of coil connected to supply...

A] remains same

B] become half

C] <u>become doubled</u>

D] become 4 times

118] Capacitance is not affected by...

A] plate area

B] distance between plates

C] dialectic material

D] <u>frequency</u>

119] The capacitive reactance of a capacitor varies...

A] directly with frequency

B] <u>inversely with frequency</u>

C] directly with applied voltage

D] inversely with applied voltage

120] A capacitor acquired 3 coulombs of charge when 6 volts are applied across it] It has a capacitance of ...

A] <u>0.5 farad</u>

B] 3 farads

C] 3 farads

D] 18 farads

121] A capacitor is connected across a 200 volt AC line, its minimum voltage rating should be...

A] 100 volts

B] 200 Volts

C] <u>300 volts</u>

D] 400 volts

122] when testing a capacitor with an ohmmeter, the meter indicates some resistance] The capacitor under test is...

A] <u>leaky</u>

B] open

C] good

D] short

123] The total capacitance of a 40 micro farad capacitor connected in series with an 80 micro farad capacitor is...

A] <u>26.7 micro farad</u>

B] 40 micro farad

C] 60.6 micro farad

D] 120 micro farad

124] For obtaining 1 micro farad capacitor from 3 nos] of 3 micro farad capacitors we have to connect...

A] all in parallel

B] <u>all in series</u>

C] 2 series and one in parallel

D] none of the above

125] In an AC series circuit having R and C the current flowing through the capacitor will be...

A] lagging the voltage

B] <u>leading the voltage</u>

C] in phase with the voltage

D] none of the above

126] If the frequency of the supply is increased in the R-C series circuit the capacitive reactance will be

A] <u>reduced</u>

B] increased

C] having no effect

D] none of the above

127] Power companies are interested in improving the power factor to
A] <u>reduce line current</u>
B] increase motor efficiency
C] increase volt-amperes
D] decrease power
128] A capacitor increases the power factor value of an AC motor load when it is connected...
A] in series with the motor
B] in series with the starter
C] <u>in parallel with the motor</u>
D] in series with the main winding
129] Normally, the power factor of an incandescent lighting circuit is..
A] 0
B] 0.5
C] 0.707
D] <u>1.0</u>
130] When resistance alone is used to determine current in an RLC series circuit, the circuit is...
A] an inductive circuit
B] a capacitive circuit
C] a combination circuit
D] <u>a resonant circuit</u>
131] Inductive reactance is directly related to..
A] resistance
B] <u>frequency</u>
C] capacitance
D] power
132] Synchronous motor when used for power factor improvement should be...
A] under excited
B] <u>over excited</u>
C] loaded
D] running at no load
133] In a RL parallel circuit, the opposition to total current is called...
A] reactance
B] resistance
C] a vector sum
D] <u>impedance</u>

134] In a AC parallel RL circuit, the power dissipated at the
A] impedance
B] resistance
C] inductance
D] capacitance
135] How much is the nominal output voltage of a carbon zinc cell?
A] 12V
B] 1.5V
C] 2.0V
D] 2.2V
136] Cells are connected in series to..
A] increase the output voltage
B] decreases the output voltage
C] decrease the internal resistance
D] increase the current capacity
54137connected in
A] series
B] parallel
C] series-parallel
D] parallel-series
138] The capacity of a cell is measured in
A] watt-hour
B] watts
C] amperes
D] ampere-hour
139] The primary cell which has the shortest shelf life is
A] carbon – zinc
B] alkaline
C] mercury
D] lithium
140] The cell which has very high energy density for given weight or
volume to
A] carbon-zinc
B] alkaline
C] mercury
D] lithium
141] A 100-Ah capacity battery should deliver a current of 8A for
approximately...

A] <u>12 h</u>
B] 8 h
C] 20 h
D] 100 h
142] When the battery is needed to be kept idle for a long time...
A] overcharge the battery
B] remove electrolyte
C] clean the plates with distilled water
D] <u>dry them and store the battery in cool dry clean place</u>
143] The active materials of the nickel iron cell are...
A] nickel hydroxide
B] powdered iron and its oxide
C] 21% solution of caustic potash
D] <u>all the above materials</u>
144] The capacity of a cell is measured in
A] watt hour
B] watts
C] amperes
D] <u>ampere-hour</u>
145] To charge a secondary cell, the system used is
A] low voltage AC
B] high voltage AC
C] AC
D] <u>DC</u>
146] What is the number of phases in a normal industrial supply system?
A] one
B] <u>three</u>
C] four
D] two
147] In a 3 phase star connected alternator, the coils have a phase difference of...
A] <u>120°</u>
B] 240°
C] 60°
D] 360°
148] Delta connection is used no one of the following
A] primary of the transmission line transformer
B] alternator winding

C] secondary of the distribution transformer

D] primary of the distribution transformer

149] Which method can be used to measure the power in a 3-phase unbalanced load system?

A] one wattmeter method

B] tow wattmeter method

C] three wattmeter method

D] three ammeter method

150] Two wattmeters can be used to measure 3-hase power in a 3-phase, 3 wire system with...

A] balanced load

B] unbalanced load

C] balanced as well as unbalanced load

D] out of balanced load

151] A single wattmeter can be used to measure power in a 3-phase system only when the load is..

A] balanaced

B] unbalanced

C] balanced as well as unbalanced load

D] constant

152] The force producing movement of the pointer in an indicating instrument is called as...

A] deflecting force

B] controlling force

C] damping force

D] distracting force

153] A permanent magnet moving coil instrument will read...

A] only AC quantities

B] only DC quantities

C] both AC and DC quantities

D] pulsating quantities

154] An instrument using gravity control will read correctly if used in..

A] vertical position only

B] horizontal position only

C] inclined position only

D] any position

155] Which one of the following damping methods is used in permanent magnet moving coil instrument?

A] air damping

B] fluid damping

C] spring damping

D] <u>eddy current damping</u>

156] Moving coil instrument works on the effect of...

A] chemical effect

B] heating effect

C] electrostatic effect

D] <u>electromagnetic effect</u>

157] The meter installed at your house to measure electrical energy is an example of...

A] indication type instrument

B] recording type instrument

C] <u>indicating as well as recording type instrument</u>

D] integrating type instrument

158].Which of the following material is preferred for permanent magnet?

A] <u>alnico</u>

B] y-alloy

C] silicon steel

D] wrought iron

159] The instrument which could be classified as absolute instrument is...

A] milli ammeter

B] micro ammeter

C] galvanometer

D] <u>tangent galvanomer</u>

160] Which of the following methods of damping is commonly used in moving iron instrument?

A] <u>Air damping</u>

B] fluid damping

C] eddy current damping

D] viscosity damping

161] The deflecting torque of a moving iron instrument is directly proportional to the..

A] current

B] <u>square of the current</u>

C] square root of the current

D] voltage

162]Which of the following is used for measuring the medium resistance directly?

A] ammeter

B] megger

C] ohmmeter

D] voltmeter

163] An ohmmeter is used for measuring the...

A] insulation resistance

B] resistance

C] current

D] potential difference

164] Which of the following components is not a part of an ohmmeter?

A] fixed resistor

B] variable resistor

C] capacitor

D] battery

165] In shunt ohmmeter, maximum deflection signifies ..

A] maximum resistance

B] minimum resistance

C] a fault in the megger

D] none of these

166].An unknown DC voltage is to be measured, which measuring range will you select first?

A] 500V

B] 50V

C] 1.5 V

D] 0.5V

167].An unknown direct current of micro ampere rating is to be measured, which measuring range will you select first?

A] 20 micro amp

B] 15 micro amp

C] 150 micro amp

D] 500 micro amp

168] A multimeter cannot measure...

A] current

B] potential difference

C] capacitance

D] resistance

169] Dynamometer type meters are used to measure...

A] only AC quantities

B] only DC quantities

C] both AC and DC

D] pulsating AC only

170] Which effect is used in wattmeter?

A] electrodynamic effect

B] thermal effect

C] chemical effect

D] electrostatic effect

171] Which of the instrument listed below operates efficiently as wattmeter in both AC and DC?

A] PMMC instrument

B] dynamometer instrument

C] hot wire instrument

D] MI instrument

172] Electrodynamic type of instrument are used commonly for the measurement of...

A] voltage

B] current

C] resistance D]

173] When the phase and neutral of the energy meter are interchanged, its disc...

A] rotates in reverse direction

B] rotates in correct direction

C] will stop

D] rotates slowly

E] rotates at high speed

174] When the disc of energy meter is rotating even without connecting any load, the error is called

A] creeping error

B] phase error

C] friction error

D] temperature error

175] AC single phase energy meters record the energy in the unit of...

A] kilowatt hours

B] number of thousands of disc rotation

C] volt amperes

D] kilo volt ampere

176] A megger measures resistance in...

A] ohms

B] hundreds of ohms

C] thousands of ohms

D] <u>millions of ohms</u>

177] A megger is exclusively designed for measuring..

A] <u>very high resistance</u>

B] very low resistance

C] ground faults in power lines

D] over loads on DC motors

178] For pipe earthing the minimum internal diameter of galvanized
iron of steel pipe required is...

A] <u>12.5 mm</u>

B] 16mm

C] 3.5 mm

D] 4 m

179] The earth conductor provides a path to ground for..

A] <u>leakage current</u>

B] over current

C] high voltage

D] circuit current

180] if the size of the circuit copper conductor is 10 sq-mm then the size
of earth conductor in G.I] wire should be...

A] 1.5 sq.mm

B] 2.5 sq.mm

C] <u>5 sq.mm</u>

D] 10 sq.mm

181] One calory is equal to,,,

A] 4187 joules

B] 418.7 joules

C] 41.87 joules

D] <u>4.187 joules</u>

182] The operating temperature range of electrical stove with bare
heating element is...

A] 300° to 400°C

B] 500° to 600°C

C] 550° to 900°C
D] 1100° to 1300°C
183] Which appliance works on heating effect of electric current?
A] incandescent lamp
B] bimetallic thermostat
C] H R C fuse
D] toaster
184] What is the size of nichrome wire for heating element of 1000 watts, 230V heater at 500°C?
A] 18 SWG
B] 20SWG
C] 24 SWG
D] 25 SWG
185] The heat proof insulating material used for heater base is...
A] mica
B] porcelain
C] asbestos
D] glass wool
186].The temperature regulating component of an automatic electric iron is...
A] heating element
B] thermostat
C] sole plate
D] pressure plate
187].The bread toasting zone temperature is about...
A] 400°C
B] 800°C
C] 260°C
D] 975°C
188] If a winding makes electrical contact with the metal case of the mixer motor the winding is...
A] grounded
B] open circuited
C] short circuited
D] loose connected
189] If the end shafts of a rotor turns blue it is an indication of...
A] scoring

B] <u>overheating</u>
C] freezing
D] burring
190] What type of motor is used in a food mixer?
A] DC shunt motor
B] <u>universal motor</u>
C] capacitor start motor
D] capacitor start and run motor
191] In what position is the motor mounted in most of the mixers?
A] <u>vertical</u>
B] horizontal
C] inclined
D] parallel
1. The S.I. unit of power is
(a) Henry
(b) coulomb
(c) <u>watt</u>
(d) watt-hour
2. Electric pressure is also called
(a) resistance
(b) power
(c) <u>voltage</u>
(d) energy
3. The substances which have a large number of free electrons and offer a low
resistance are called
(a) insulators
(b) inductors
(c) semi-conductors
(d) <u>conductors</u>
4. Out of the following which is not a poor conductor ?
(a) Cast iron
(b) <u>Copper</u>
(c) Carbon
(d) Tungsten
5. Out of the following which is an insulating material ?
(a) Copper
(b) Gold

(c) Silver

(d) <u>Paper</u>

6. The property of a conductor due to which it passes current is called

(a) resistance

(b) reluctance

(c) <u>conductance</u>

(d) inductance

7. Conductance is reciprocal of

(a) <u>resistance</u>

(b) inductance

(c) reluctance

(d) capacitance

8. The resistance of a conductor varies inversely as

(a) length

(b) <u>area of cross-section</u>

(c) temperature

(d) resistivity

9. With rise in temperature the resistance of pure metals

(a) <u>increases</u>

(b) decreases

(c) first increases and then decreases

(d) remains constant

10. With rise in temperature the resistance of semi-conductors

(a) <u>decreases</u>

(b) increases

(c) first increases and then decreases

(d) remains constant

11. The resistance of a copper wire 200 m long is 21 Q. If its thickness (diameter)

is 0.44 mm, its specific resistance is around

(a) $1.2 \times 10^{\sim}8$ Q-m

(b) $1.4 \times 10^{\sim}8$ Q-m

(c) <u>$1.6 \times 10^{""}8$ Q-m</u>

(d) $1.8 \times 10^{"}8$ Q-m

13. An instrument which detects electric current is known as

(a) voltmeter

(b) rheostat

(c) wattmeter

(d) <u>galvanometer</u>

14. In a circuit a 33 Q resistor carries a current of 2 A. The voltage across the resistor is

(a) 33 V

(b) <u>66 v</u>

(c) 80 V

(d) 132 V

15. A light bulb draws 300 mA when the voltage across it is 240 V. The resistance of the light bulb is

(a) 400 Q

(b) 600 Q

(c) <u>800 Q</u>

(d) 1000 Q

16. The resistance of a parallel circuit consisting of two branches is 12 ohms. If the resistance of one branch is 18 ohms, what is the resistance of the other ?

(a) 18 Q

(b) <u>36 Q</u>

(c) 48 Q

(d) 64 Q

17. Four wires of same material, the same cross-sectional area and the same length when connected in parallel give a resistance of 0.25 Q. If the same four wires are connected is series the effective resistance will be

(a) 1 Q

(b) 2 Q

(c) 3 Q

(d) <u>4 Q</u>

18. A current of 16 amperes divides between two branches in parallel of resistances 8 ohms and 12 ohms respectively. The current in each branch is

(a) 6.4 A, 6.9 A

(b) <u>6.4 A, 9.6 A</u>

(c) 4.6 A, 6.9 A

(d) 4.6 A, 9.6 A

19. Current velocity through a copper conductor is

(a) the same as propagation velocity of electric energy

(b) independent of current strength

(c) <u>of the order of a few ^.s/m</u>

(d) nearly 3 x 108 m/s

20. Which of the following material has nearly zero temperature co-efficient of resistance?

(a) <u>Manganin</u>

(b) Porcelain

(c) Carbon

(d) Copper

21. You have to replace 1500 Q resistor in radio. You have no 1500 Q resistor but have several 1000 Q ones which you would connect

(a) two in parallel

(b) <u>two in parallel and one in series</u>

(c) three in parallel

(d) three in series

22. Two resistors are said to be connected in series when

(a) <u>same current passes in turn through both</u>

(b) both carry the same value of current

(c) total current equals the sum of branch currents

(d) sum of IR drops equals the applied e.m.f.

23. Which of the following statement is true both for a series and a parallel D.C. circuit?

(a) Elements have individual currents

(b) Currents are additive

(c) Voltages are additive

(d) <u>Power are additive</u>

24. Which of the following materials has a negative temperature co-efficient of resistance?

(a) Copper

(b) Aluminum

(c) <u>Carbon</u>

(d) Brass

25. Ohm's law is not applicable to

(a) <u>vacuum tubes</u>

(b) carbon resistors

(c) high voltage circuits

(d) circuits with low current densities

26. Which is the best conductor of electricity ?

(a) Iron

(b) <u>Silver</u>

(c) Copper

(d) Carbon

27. For which of the following 'ampere second' could be the unit ?

(a) Reluctance

(b) <u>Charge</u>

(c) Power

(d) Energy

28. All of the following are equivalent to watt except

(a) (amperes) ohm

(b) joules/sec.

(c) amperes x volts

(d) <u>amperes/volt</u>

29. A resistance having rating 10 ohms, 10 W is likely to be a

(a) metallic resistor

(b) carbon resistor

(c) <u>wire wound resistor</u>

(d) variable resistor

30. Which one of the following does not have negative temperature co-efficient ?

(a) <u>Aluminium</u>

(b) Paper

(c) Rubber

(d) Mica

31. Varistors are

(a) insulators

(6) <u>non-linear resistors</u>

(c) carbon resistors

(d) resistors with zero temperature coefficient

32. Insulating materials have the function of

(a) preventing a short circuit between conducting wires

(b) <u>preventing an open circuit between the voltage source and the load</u>

(c) conducting very large currents

(d) storing very high currents

33. The rating of a fuse wire is always expressed in

(a) ampere-hours

(b) ampere-volts

(c) kWh

(d) <u>amperes</u>

34. The minimum charge on an ion is

(a) equal to the atomic number of the atom

(b) <u>equal to the charge of an electron</u>

(c) equal to the charge of the number of electrons in an atom (#) zero

35. In a series circuit with unequal resistances

(a) the highest resistance has the most of the current through it

(b) the lowest resistance has the highest voltage drop

(c) the lowest resistance has the highest current

(d) <u>the highest resistance has the highest voltage drop</u>

36. The filament of an electric bulb is made of

(a) carbon

(b) aluminium

(c) tungsten

(d) nickel

37. A 3 Q resistor having 2 A current will dissipate the power of

(a) 2 watts

(b) 4 watts

(c) <u>6 watts</u>

(d) 8 watts

38. Which of the following statement is true?

(a) A galvanometer with low resistance in parallel is a voltmeter

(b) A galvanometer with high resistance in parallel is a voltmeter

(c) <u>A galvanometer resistance in series is an ammeter with low</u>

(d) A galvanometer with high resistance in series is an ammeter

39. The resistance of a few meters of wire conductor in closed electrical circuit is

(a) <u>practically zero</u>

(b) low

(c) high

(d) very high

40. If a parallel circuit is opened in the main line, the current

(a) increases in the branch of the lowest resistance

(b) increases in each branch

(c) <u>is zero in all branches</u>

(d) is zero in the highest resistive branch

41. If a wire conductor of 0.2 ohm resistance is doubled in length, its resistance becomes

(a) <u>0.4 ohm</u>

(b) 0.6 ohm

(c) 0.8 ohm

(d) 1.0 ohm

42. Three 60 W bulbs are in parallel across the 60 V power line. If one bulb burns open

(a) there will be heavy current in the main line

(b) rest of the two bulbs will not light

(c) all three bulbs will light

(d) the other two bulbs will light

43. The four bulbs of 40 W each are connected in series swift a battery across them, which of the following statement is true ?

(a) The current through each bulb in same

(b) The voltage across each bulb is not same

(c) The power dissipation in each bulb is not same

(d) None of the above

44. Two resistances Rl and Ri are connected in series across the voltage source where Rl>Ri. The largest drop will be across

(a) Rl

(b) Ri

(c) either Rl or Ri

(d) none of them

46. A closed switch has a resistance of

(a) zero

(b) about 50 ohms

(c) about 500 ohms

(d) infinity

47. The hot resistance of the bulb's filament is higher than its cold resistance because the temperature co-efficient of the filament is

(a) zero

(b) negative

(c) positive

(d) about 2 ohms per degree

49. The insulation on a current carrying conductor is provided

(a) to prevent leakage of current

(b) to prevent shock

(c) both of above factors

(d) none of above factors

50. The thickness of insulation provided on the conductor depends on

(a) the magnitude of voltage on the conductor

(b) the magnitude of current flowing through it

(c) both (a) and (b)

(d) none of the above

51. Which of the following quantities remain the same in all parts of a series circuit ?

(a) Voltage

(b) <u>Current</u>

(c) Power

(d) Resistance

52. A 40 W bulb is connected in series with a room heater. If now 40 W bulb is replaced by 100 W bulb, the heater output will

(a) decrease

(b) <u>increase</u>

(c) remain same

(d) heater will burn out

53. In an electric kettle water boils in 10 m minutes. It is required to boil the boiler in 15 minutes, using same supply mains

(a) <u>length of heating element should be decreased</u>

(b) length of heating element should be increased

(c) length of heating element has no effect on heating if water

(d) none of the above

54. An electric filament bulb can be worked from

(a) D.C. supply only

(b) A.C. supply only

(c) Battery supply only

(d) <u>All above</u>

55. Resistance of a tungsten lamp as applied voltage increases

(a) decreases

(b) <u>increases</u>

(c) remains same

(d) none of the above

56. Electric current passing through the circuit produces

(a) magnetic effect

(b) luminous effect

(c) <u>thermal effect</u>

(d) chemical effect

(e) all above effects

57. Resistance of a material always decreases if

(a) temperature of material is decreased

(6) temperature of material is increased

(c) number of free electrons available become more

(d) none of the above is correct

58. If the efficiency of a machine is to be high, what should be low ?

(a) Input power

(b) <u>Losses</u>

(c) True component of power

(d) kWh consumed

(e) Ratio of output to input

59. When electric current passes through a metallic conductor, its temperature rises. This is due to

(a) <u>collisions between conduction electrons and atoms</u>

(b) the release of conduction electrons from parent atoms

(c) mutual collisions between metal atoms

(d) mutual collisions between conducting electrons

60. Two bulbs of 500 W and 200 W rated at 250 V will have resistance ratio as

(a) 4 : 25

(b) 25 : 4

(c) <u>2 : 5</u>

(d) 5 : 2

61. A glass rod when rubbed with silk cloth is charged because

(a) it takes in proton

(b) its atoms are removed

(c) <u>it gives away electrons</u>

(d) it gives away positive charge

62. Whether circuit may be AC. or D.C. one, following is most effective in

reducing the magnitude of the current.

(a) Reactor

(b) Capacitor

(c) Inductor

(d) <u>Resistor</u>

63. It becomes more difficult to remove

(a) any electron from the orbit

(6) first electron from the orbit

(c) second electron from the orbit

(d) <u>third electron from the orbit</u>

64. When one leg of parallel circuit is opened out the total current will

(a) reduce

(b) increase

(c) <u>decrease</u>

(d) become zero

65. In a lamp load when more than one lamp are switched on the total resistance

of the load

(a) increases

(b) <u>decreases</u>

(c) remains same

(d) none of the above

66. Two lamps 100 W and 40 W are connected in series across 230 V (alternating).

Which of the following statement is correct ?

(a) 100 W lamp will glow brighter

(b) <u>40 W lamp will glow brighter</u>

(c) Both lamps will glow equally bright

(d) 40 W lamp will fuse

67. Resistance of 220 V, 100 W lamp will be

(a) 4.84 Q

(b) 48.4 Q

(c) <u>484 ft</u>

(d) 4840 Q

68. In the case of direct current

(a) <u>magnitude and direction of current remains constant</u>

(b) magnitude and direction of current changes with time

(c) magnitude of current changes with time

(d) magnitude of current remains constant

69. When electric current passes through a bucket full of water, lot of bubbling is

observed. This suggests that the type of supply is

(a) A.C.

(b) <u>D.C.</u>

(c) any of above two

(d) none of the above

70. Resistance of carbon filament lamp as the applied voltage increases.

(a) increases
(b) decreases
(c) remains same
(d) none of the above
71. Bulbs in street lighting are all connected in
(a) parallel
(b) series
(c) series-parallel
(d) end-to-end
72. For testing appliances, the wattage of test lamp should be
(a) very low
(b) low
(c) high
(d) any value
73. Switching of a lamp in house produces noise in the radio. This is because switching operation produces
(a) arcs across separating contacts
(b) mechanical noise of high intensity
(c) both mechanical noise and arc between contacts
(d) none of the above
74. Sparking occurs when a load is switched off because the circuit has high
(a) resistance
(b) inductance
(c) capacitance
(d) impedance
75. Copper wire of certain length and resistance is drawn out to three times its
length without change in volume, the new resistance of wire becomes
(a) 1/9 times
(b) 3 times
(c) 9 times
(d) unchanged
76. When resistance element of a heater fuses and then we reconnect it after removing a portion of it, the power of the heater will
(a) decrease
(b) increase
(c) remain constant

(d) none of the above

77. A field of force can exist only between

(a) two molecules

(b) two ions

(c) two atoms

(d) two metal particles

78. A substance whose molecules consist of dissimilar atoms is called

(a) semi-conductor

(b) super-conducto

(c) compound

(d) insulator

79. International ohm is defined in terms of the resistance of

(a) a column of mercury

(b) a cube of carbon

(c) a cube of copper

(d) the unit length of wire

80. Three identical resistors are first connected in parallel and then in series.

The resultant resistance of the first combination to the second will be

(a) 9 times

(b) 1/9 times

(c) 1/3 times

(d) 3 times

91. Which method can be used for absolute measurement of resistances ?

(a) Lorentz method

(b) Releigh method

(c) Ohm's law method

(d) Wheatstone bridge method

92. Three 6 ohm resistors are connected to form a triangle. What is the resistance between any two corners ?

(a) 3/2 Q

(b 6 Q

(c) 4 Q

(d) 8/3 Q

93. Ohm's law is not applicable to

(a) semi-conductors

(b) D.C. circuits

(c) small resistors

(d) high currents

94. Two copper conductors have equal length. The cross-sectional area of one conductor is four times that of the other. If the conductor having smaller crosssectional area has a resistance of 40 ohms the resistance of other conductor will be

(a) 160 ohms

(b) 80 ohms

(c) 20 ohms

(d) <u>10 ohms</u>

95. A nichrome wire used as a heater coil has the resistance of 2 £2/m. For a heater of 1 kW at 200 V, the length of wire required will be

(a) <u>80 m</u>

(b) 60 m

(c) 40 m

(d) 20 m

96. Temperature co-efficient of resistance is expressed in terms of

(a) ohms/°C

(b) mhos/ohm°C

(c) <u>ohms/ohm°C</u>

98. When current flows through heater coil it glows but supply wiring does not glow because

(a) current through supply line flows at slower speed

(b) supply wiring is covered with insulation layer

(c) <u>resistance of heater coil is more than the supply wires</u>

(d) supply wires are made of superior material

99. The condition for the validity under Ohm's law is that

(a) <u>resistance must be uniform</u>

(b) current should be proportional to the size of the resistance

(c) resistance must be wire wound type

(d) temperature at positive end should be more than the temperature at negative end

100. Which of the following statement is correct ?

(a) <u>A semi-conductor is a material whose conductivity is same as between that of a conductor and an insulator</u>

(b) A semi-conductor is a material which has conductivity having average value of conductivity of metal and insulator

(c) A semi-conductor is one which con¬ducts only half of the applied voltage

(d) A semi-conductor is a material made of alternate layers of conducting material and insulator

101. A rheostat differs from potentiometer in the respect that it

(a) has lower wattage rating

(b) has higher wattage rating

(c) has large number of turns

(d) offers large number of tapping

102. The weight of an aluminium conductor as compared to a copper conductor of identical cross-section, for the same electrical resistance, is

(a) 50%

(b) 60%

(c) 100%

(d) 150%

103. An open resistor, when checked with an ohm-meter reads

(a) zero

(b) infinite

(c) high but within tolerance

(d) low but not zero

104. are the materials having electrical conductivity much less than most of the metals but much greater than that of typical insulators.

(a) Varistors

(b) Thermistor

(c) Semi-conductors

(d) Variable resistors

105. All good conductors have high

(a) conductance

(b) resistance

(c) reluctance

(d) thermal conductivity

106. Voltage dependent resistors are usually made from

(a) charcoal

(b) silicon carbide

(c) nichrome

(d) graphite

107. Voltage dependent resistors are used

(a) for inductive circuits

(b) <u>to supress surges</u>

(c) as heating elements

(d) as current stabilizers

108. The ratio of mass of proton to that of electron is nearly

(a) <u>1840</u>

(b) 1840

(c) 30

(d) 4

109. The number of electrons in the outer most orbit of carbon atom is

(a) 3

(b) <u>4</u>

(c) 6

(d) 7

110. With three resistances connected in parallel, if each dissipates 20 W
the total power supplied by the voltage source equals

(a) 10 W

(b) 20 W

(c) 40 W

(d) <u>60 W</u>

111. A thermistor has

(a) positive temperature coefficient

(b) negative temperature coefficient

(c) <u>zero temperature coefficient</u>

(d) variable temperature coefficient

112. If/, R and t are the current, resistance and time respectively, then
according

to Joule's law heat produced will be proportional to

(a) <u>I2Rt</u>

(b) I2Rf

(c) I2R2t

(d) I2R2t*

113. Nichrome wire is an alloy of

(a) lead and zinc

(b) chromium and vanadium

(c) <u>nickel and chromium</u>

(d) copper and silver

114. When a voltage of one volt is applied, a circuit allows one micro
ampere current to flow through it. The conductance of the circuit is

(a) <u>1 n-mho</u>
(b) 106 mho
(c) 1 milli-mho
(d) none of the above
115. Which of the following can have negative temperature coefficient ?
(a) Compounds of silver
(6) Liquid metals
(c) Metallic alloys
(d) <u>Electrolytes</u>
116. Conductance : mho ::
(a) <u>resistance : ohm</u>
(b) capacitance : henry
(c) inductance : farad
(d) lumen : steradian
117. 1 angstrom is equal to
(a) 10-8 mm
(b) 10"6 cm
(c) <u>10"10 m</u>
(d) 10~14 m
118. One newton meter is same as
(a) one watt
(b) <u>one joule</u>
(c) five joules
(d) one joule second
1. The property of coil by which a counter e.m.f. is induced in it when the current
through the coil changes is known as
(a) <u>self-inductance</u>
(b) mutual inductance
(c) series aiding inductance
(d) capacitance
2. As per Faraday's laws of electromagnetic induction, an e.m.f. is induced in a
conductor whenever it
(a) lies perpendicular to the magnetic flux
(b) lies in a magnetic field
(c) <u>cuts magnetic flux</u>
(d) moves parallel to the direction of the magnetic field

3. Which of the following circuit element stores energy in the electromagnetic

field ?

(a) <u>Inductance</u>

(b) Condenser

(c) Variable resistor

(d) Resistance

4. The inductance of a coil will increase under all the following conditions except

(a) <u>when more length for the same number of turns is provided</u>

(6) when the number of turns of the coil increase

(c) when more area for each turn is provided

(d) when permeability of the core increases

5. Higher the self-inductance of a coil,

(a) lesser its weber-turns

(b) lower the e.m.f. induced

(c) greater the flux produced by it

(d) <u>longer the delay in establishing steady current through it</u>

6. In an iron cored coil the iron core is removed so that the coil becomes an air cored coil. The inductance of the coil will

(a) increase

(b) <u>decrease</u>

(c) remain the same

(d) initially increase and then decrease

7. An open coil has

(a) zero resistance and inductance

(b) <u>infinite resistance and zero inductance</u>

(c) infinite resistance and normal inductance

(d) zero resistance and high inductance

8. Both the number of turns and the core length of an inductive coil are doubled.

Its self-inductance will be

(a) unaffected

(b) <u>doubled</u>

(c) halved

(d) quadrupled

9. If current in a conductor increases then according to Lenz's law self-induced

voltage will

(a) aid the increasing current

(b) tend to decrease the amount of cur-rent

(c) <u>produce current opposite to the in-creasing current</u>

(d) aid the applied voltage

10. The direction of induced e.m.f. can be found by

(a) Laplace's law

(b) <u>Lenz's law</u>

(c) Fleming's right hand rule

(d) Kirchhoff s voltage law

11. Air-core coils are practically free from

(a) hysteresis losses

(b) eddy current losses

(c) <u>both (a) and (b)</u>

(d) none of the above

12. The magnitude of the induced e.m.f. in a conductor depends on the

(a) flux density of the magnetic field

(b) amount of flux cut

(c) amount of flux linkages

(d) <u>rate of change of flux-linkages</u>

13. Mutually inductance between two magnetically-coupled coils depends on

(a) permeability of the core

(b) the number of their turns

(c) cross-sectional area of their common core

(d) <u>all of the above</u>

14. A laminated iron core has reduced eddy-current losses because

(a) more wire can be used with less D.C. resistance in coil

(b) <u>the laminations are insulated from each other</u>

(c) the magnetic flux is concentrated in the air gap of the core

(d) the laminations are stacked vertfcally

15. The law that the induced e.m.f. and current always oppose the cause producing them is due to

(a) Faraday

(b) <u>Lenz</u>

(c) Newton

16. Which of the following is not a unit of inductance ?

(a) Henry

(b) <u>Coulomb/volt ampere</u>

(c) Volt second per ampere

(d) All of the above

17. In case of an inductance, current is proportional to

(a) voltage across the inductance

(b) <u>magnetic field</u>

(c) both (a) and (b)

(d) neither (a) nor (b)

18. Which of the following circuit elements will oppose the change in circuit current ?

(a) Capacitance

(b) <u>Inductance</u>

(c) Resistance

(d) All of the above

19. For a purely inductive circuit which of the following is true ?

(a) Apparent power is zero

(b) Relative power is.zero

(c) <u>Actual power of the circuit is zero</u>

(d) Any capacitance even if present in the circuit will not be charged

20. Which of the following is unit of inductance ?

(a) Ohm

(b) <u>Henry</u>

(c) Ampere turns

(d) Webers/metre

21. An e.m.f. of 16 volts is induced in a coil of inductance 4H. The rate of change of current must be

(a) 64 A/s

(b) 32 A/s

(c) 16 A/s

(d) <u>4 A/s</u>

22. The core of a coil has a length of 200 mm. The inductance of coil is 6 mH. If the core length is doubled, all other quantities, remaining the same, the inductance will be

(a) <u>3 mH</u>

(b) 12 mH

(c) 24mH

(d)48mH

23. The self inductances of two coils are 8 mH and 18 mH. If the co-efficients of coupling is 0.5, the mutual inductance of the coils is

(a) 4 mH

(b) 5 mH

(c) <u>6 mH</u>

(d) 12 mH

24. Two coils have inductances of 8 mH and 18 mH and a co-efficient of coupling of 0.5. If the two coils are connected in series aiding, the total inductance will be

(a) 32 mH

(b) <u>38 mH</u>

(c) 40 mH

(d) 48 mH

25. A 200 turn coil has an inductance of 12 mH. If the number of turns is increased to 400 turns, all other quantities (area, length etc.) remaining the same, the inductance will be

(a) 6 mH

(b) 14 mH

(c) 24 mH

(d) <u>48 mH</u>

26. Two coils have self-inductances of 10 H and 2 H, the mutual inductance being zero. If the two coils are connected in series, the total inductance will be

(a) 6 H

(b) 8 H

(c) <u>12 H</u>

(d) 24 H

27. In case all the flux from the current in coil 1 links with coil 2, the co-efficient of coupling will be

(a) 2.0

(b) <u>1.0</u>

(c) 0.5

(d) zero

28. A coil with negligible resistance has 50V across it with 10 mA. The inductive

reactance is

(a) 50 ohms

(b) 500 ohms

(c) 1000 ohms

(d) <u>5000 ohms</u>

29. A conductor 2 meters long moves at right angles to a magnetic field of flux density 1 tesla with a velocity of 12.5 m/s. The induced e.m.f. in the conductor will be

(a) 10 V

(6) 15 V

(c) <u>25V</u>

(d) 50V

30. Lenz's law is a consequence of the law of conservation of

(a) induced current

(b) charge

(c) <u>energy</u>

(d) induced e.m.f.

31. A conductor carries 125 amperes of current under 60° to a magnetic field of 1.1 tesla. The force on the conductor will be

nearly

(a) 50 N

(b) <u>120 N</u>

(c) 240 N

(d) 480 N

32. Find the force acting on a conductor 3m long carrying a current of 50 amperes at right angles to a magnetic field having a flux density of 0.67 tesla.

(a) <u>100 N</u>

(b) 400 N

(c) 600 N

(d) 1000 N

33. The co-efficient of coupling between two air core coils depends on

(a) self-inductance of two coils only

(b) mutual inductance between two coils only

(c) <u>mutual inductance and self inductance of two coils</u>

(d) none of the above

34. An average voltage of 10 V is induced in a 250 turns solenoid as a result of a change in flux which occurs in 0.5 second. The total flux change is

(a) 20 Wb

(b) 2 Wb

(c) 0.2 Wb

(d) <u>0.02 Wb</u>

35. A 500 turns solenoid develops an average induced voltage of 60 V. Over what time interval must a flux change of 0.06 Wb occur to produce such a voltage ?

(a) 0.01 s

(b) 0.1 s

(c) <u>0.5 s</u>

(d) 5 s

36. Which of the fpllowing inductor will have the least eddy current losses ?

(a) <u>Air core</u>

(b) Laminated iron core

(c) Iron core

(d) Powdered iron core

37. A coil induces 350 mV when the current changes at the rate of 1 A/ s. The value of inductance is

(a) 3500 mH

(b) <u>350 mH</u>

(c) 250 mH

(d) 150 mH

38. Two 300 uH coils in series without mutual coupling have a total inductance of

(a) 300 uH

(b) <u>600 uH</u>

(c) 150 uH

(d) 75 uH

39. Current changing from 8 A to 12 A in one second induced 20 volts in a coil. The value of inductance is

(a) 5 mH

(b) 10 mH

(c) <u>5 H</u>

(d) 10 H

40. Which circuit element(s) will oppose the change in circuit current ?

(a) Resistance only

(b) <u>Inductance only</u>

(c) Capacitance only

(d) Inductance and capacitance

41. A crack in the magnetic path of an inductor will result in

(a) unchanged inductance

(b) increased inductance

(c) zero inductance

(d) <u>reduced inductance</u>

42. A coil is wound on iron core which carries current I. The self-induced voltage in the coil is not affected by

(a) variation in coil current

(b) <u>variation in voltage to the coil</u>

(c) change of number of turns of coil

(d) the resistance of magnetic path

1. A transistor has ....

A] one pn junction

B] <u>two pn junctions</u>

C] three pn junctions

D] four pn junctions

2. The number of depletion layers in a transistor is ....

A] four

B] three

C] one

D] <u>two</u>

3. The base of a transistor is .... doped

A] heavily

B] moderately

C] <u>lightly</u>

D] none of the above

4. The element that has the biggest size in a transistor is ....

A] <u>collector</u>

B] base

C] emitter

D] collector-base-junction

5. In a pnp transistor, the current carriers are ....

A] acceptor ions

B] donor ions

C] free electrons

D] <u>holes</u>

6. The collector of a transistor is .... doped

A] heavily

B] <u>moderately</u>
C] lightly
D] none of the above
7. A transistor is a .... operated device
A] <u>current</u>
B] voltage
C] both voltage and current
D] none of the above
8. In a npn transistor, ... are the minority carriers
A] free electrons
B] <u>holes</u>
C] donor ions
D] acceptor ions
9. The emitter of a transistor is .... doped
A] lightly
B] <u>heavily</u>
C] moderately
D] none of the above
10. In a transistor, the base current is about .... of emitter current
A] 25%
B] 20%
C] 35 %
D] <u>5%</u>
11. At the base-emitter junctions of a transistor, one finds ....
A] a reverse bias
B] a wide depletion layer
C] <u>low resistance</u>
D] none of the above
12. The input impedance of a transistor is ....
A] high
B] <u>low</u>
C] very high
D] almost zero
13. Most of the majority carriers from the emitter ....
A] recombine in the base
B] recombine in the emitter
C] <u>pass through the base region to the collector</u>
D] none of the above

14. The current IB is ....
A] <u>electron current</u>
B] hole current
C] donor ion current
D] acceptor ion current
15. In a transistor ....
A] IC = IE + IB
B] IB = IC + IE
C] IE = IC – IB
D] <u>IE = IC + IB</u>
16. The value of a of a transistor is ....
A] more than 1
B] <u>less than 1</u>
C] 1
D] none of the above
17. IC = aIE + ...
A] IB
B] ICEO
C] <u>ICBO</u>
D] ßIB
18. The output impedance of a transistor is ....
A] <u>high</u>
B] zero
C] low
D] very low
19. In a tansistor, IC = 100 mA and IE = 100.2 mA. The value of ß is
....
A] 100
B] 50
C] about 1
D] <u>200</u>
20. In a transistor if ß = 100 and collector current is 10 mA, then IE
is ....
A] 100 mA
B] <u>100.1 mA</u>
C] 110 mA
D] none of the above
21. The relation between ß and a is ....

A] ß = 1 / (1 – a)
B] ß = (1 – a) / a
C] ß = a / (1 – a)
D] ß = a / (1 + a)
22. The value of ß for a transistor is generally ....
A] 1less than 1
B] between 20 and 500
C] above 500
23. The most commonly used transistor arrangement is ....
arrangement
A] common emitter
B] common base
C] common collector
D] none of the above
24. The input impedance of a transistor connected in
.................arrangement is the highest
A] common emitter
B] common collector
C] common base
D] none of the above
25. The output impedance of a transistor connected in ....
A] arrangement is the highest
B] common emitter
C] common collector
D] common base
none of the above
26. The phase difference between the input and output voltages in a
common base arrangement is ....
A] 180o
B] 90o
C] 270o
D] 0o
27. The power gain in a transistor connected in .... arrangement is
the highest
A] common emitter
B] common base
C] common collector
D] none of the above

28. The phase difference between the input and output voltages of a transistor connected in common emitter arrangement is ....

A] 0o

B] <u>180o</u>

C] 90o

D] 270o

29. The voltage gain in a transistor connected in .... arrangement is the highest

A] common base

B] common collector

C] <u>common emitter</u>

D] none of the above

30. As the temperature of a transistor goes up, the base-emitter resistance ....

A] <u>decreases</u>

B] increases

C] remains the same

D] none of the above

31. The voltage gain of a transistor connected in common collector

A] arrangement is ....

B] equal to 1

C] more than 10

D] <u>more than 100 less than 1</u>

32. The phase difference between the input and output voltages of a transistor connected in common collector arrangement is ....

A] 180o

B] <u>0o</u>

C] 90o

D] 270o

33. IC = ß IB + ...

A] ICBO

B] IC

C] <u>ICEO</u>

D] aIE

34. IC = [a / (1 – a)] IB + ...

A] <u>ICEO</u>

B] ICBO

C] IC

D] (1 – a) IB

35. IC = [a / (1 – a)] IB + [........ / (1 – a)]

A] ICBO

B] ICEO

C] IC

D] IE

36. BC 147 transistor indicates that it is made of ....

A] germanium

B] silicon

C] carbon

D] none of the above

37. ICEO = (.........) ICBO

A] ß1

B] + a

C] 1 + ß

D] none of the above

38. A transistor is connected in CB mode. If it is not connected in CE mode with same bias voltages, the values of IE, IB and IC will ....

A] remain the same

B] increase

C] decrease

D] none of the above

39. If the value of a is 0.9, then value of ß is ....

A] 9

B] 0.9

C] 900

D] 90

40. In a transistor, signal is transferred from a .... circuit

A] high resistance to low resistance

B] low resistance to high resistance

C] high resistance to high resistance

D] low resistance to low resistance

41. The arrow in the symbol of a transistor indicates the direction of ....

A] electron current in the emitter

B] electron current in the collector

C] hole current in the emitter

D] donor ion current

42. The leakage current in CE arrangement is .... that in CB arrangement

A] <u>more than</u>

B] less than

C] the same as

D] none of the above

43. A heat sink is generally used with a transistor to ....

A] increase the forward current

B] decrease the forward current

C] compensate for excessive doping

D] <u>prevent excessive temperature rise</u>

44. The most commonly used semiconductor in the manufacture of a transistor is ....

A] germanium

B] <u>silicon</u>

C] carbon

D] none of the above

45. The collector-base junction in a transistor has ....

A] forward bias at all times

B] <u>reverse bias at all times</u>

C] low resistance

D] none of the above

1. A tuned amplifier uses .... load

A] Resistive

B] Capacitive

C] <u>LC tank</u>

D] Inductive

2. A tuned amplifier is generally operated in .... operation

A] Class A

B] <u>Class C</u>

C] Class B

D] None of the above

3. A tuned amplifier is used in .... applications

A] <u>Radio frequency</u>

B] Low frequency

C] Audio frequency

D] None of the above

4. Frequencies above .... kHz are called radio frequencies

A] 21

B] 0

C] 50

D] 200

6. The voltage gain of a tuned amplifier is .... at resonant frequency

A] Minimum

B] Maximum

C] Half-way between maximum and minimum

D] Zero

7. At parallel resonance, the line current is ....

A] Minimum

B] Maximum

C] Quite large

D] None of the above

8. At series resonance, the circuit offers .... impedance

A] Zero

B] Maximum

C] Minimum

D] None of the above

9. A resonant circuit contains .... elements

A] R and L only

B] R and C only

C] Only R

D] L and C

10. At series or parallel resonance, the circuit behaves as a .... load

A] Capacitive

B] Resistive

C] Inductive

D] None of the above

11. At series resonance, voltage across L is .... voltage across C

A] Equal to but opposite in phase to

B] Equal to but in phase with

C] Greater than but in phase with

D] Less than but in phase with

12. When either L or C is increased, the resonant frequency of LC circuit ....

A] Remains the same

B] Increases

C] <u>Decreases</u>

D] Insufficient data

13. At parallel resonance, the net reactive component circuit current is ....

A] Capacitive

B] <u>Zero</u>

C] Inductive

D] None of the above

14. In parallel resonance, the circuit impedance is ....

A] C/LR

B] R/LC

C] CR/L

D] <u>L/CR</u>

15. In a parallel LC circuit, if the input signal frequency is increased above resonant frequency then ....

A] <u>XL increases and XC decreases</u>

B] XL decreases and XC increases

C] Both XL and XC increase

D] Both XL and XC decrease

16. The Q of an LC circuit is given by ....

A] 2pfr x R

B] R / 2pfrL

C] <u>2pfrL / R</u>

D] R2/2pfrL

17. If Q of an LC circuit increases, then bandwidth ....

A] Increases

B] <u>Decreases</u>

C] Remains the same

D] Insufficient data

18. At series resonance, the net reactive component of circuit current is ....

A] <u>Zero</u>

B] Inductive

C] Capacitive

D] None of the above

19. The dimensions of L/CR are that of ....

A] Farad

B] Henry

C] <u>Ohm</u>

D] None of the above

20. If L/C ratio of a parallel LC circuit is increased, the Q of the circuit ....

A] Is decreased

B] <u>Is increased</u>

C] Remains the same

D] None of the above

21. At series resonance, the phase angle between applied voltage and circuit is ....

A] 90o

B] 180o

C] <u>0o</u>

D] None of the above

22. At parallel resonance, the ratio L/C is ....

A] <u>Very large</u>

B] Zero

C] Small

D] None of the above

23. If the resistance of a tuned circuit is increased, the Q of the circuit ....

A] Is increased

B] <u>Is decreased</u>

C] Remains the same

D] None of the above

24. The Q of a tuned circuit refers to the property of ....

A] Sensitivity

B] Fidelity

C] <u>Selectivity</u>

D] None of the above

25. At parallel resonance, the phase angle between the applied voltage and circuit current is ....

A] 90o

B] 180o

C] <u>0o</u>

D] None of the above

26. In a parallel LC circuit, if the signal frequency is decreased below the resonant frequency, then ....

A] <u>XL decreases and XC increases</u>

B] XL increases and XC decreases

C] Line current becomes minimum

D] None of the above

27. In series resonance, there is ....

A] <u>Voltage amplification</u>

B] Current amplification

C] Both voltage and current amplification

D] None of the above

28. The Q of a tuned amplifier is generally ....

A] Less than 5

B] Less than 10

C] <u>More than 10</u>

D] None of the above

29. The Q of a tuned amplifier is 50. If the resonant frequency for the amplifier is 1000kHZ, then bandwidth is ....

A] 10kHz

B] 40 kHz

C] 30 kHz

D] <u>20 kHz</u>

30. In the above question, what are the values of cut-off frequencies?

A] 140 kHz , 60 kHz

B] <u>1020 kHz , 980 kHz</u>

C] 1030 kHz , 970 kHz

D] None of the above

31. For frequencies above the resonant frequency, a parallel LC circuit behaves as a .... load

A] <u>Capacitive</u>

B] Resistive

C] Inductive

D] None of the above

32. In parallel resonance, there is ....

A] Both voltage and current amplification

B] Voltage amplifications

C] <u>Current amplification</u>

D] None of the above

33. For frequencies below resonant frequency, a series LC circuit behaves as a .... load

A] Resistive

B] <u>Capacitive</u>

C] Inductive

D] None of the above

34. If a high degree of selectivity is desired, then double-tuned circuit should have .... coupling

A] <u>Loose</u>

B] Tight

C] Critical

D] None of the above

35. In the double tuned circuit, if the mutual inductance between the two tuned circuits is decreased, the level of resonance curve ....

A] Remains the same

B] Is lowered

C] <u>Is raised</u>

D] None of the above

36. For frequencies above the resonant frequency , a series LC circuit behaves as a .... load

A] Resistive

B] <u>Inductive</u>

C] Capacitive

D] None of the above

37. Double tuned circuits are used in .... stages of a radio receiver

A] <u>IF</u>

B] Audio

C] Output

D] None of the above

38. A class C amplifier always drives .... load

A] A pure resistive

B] A pure inductive

C] A pure capacitive

D] <u>A resonant tank</u>

39. Tuned class C amplifiers are used for RF signals of ....

A] Low power

B] High power

C] Very high power

D] <u>None of the above</u>

40. For frequencies below the resonant frequency , a parallel LC circuit behaves as a .... load

A] <u>Inductive</u>

B] Resistive

C] Capacitive

D] None of the above

1. A radio receiver has .... of amplification

A] One stage

B] Two stages

C] Three stages

D] <u>More than one stages</u>

2. RC coupling is used for .... amplification

A] <u>Voltage</u>

B] Current

C] Power

D] None of the above

3. In an RC coupled amplifier, the voltage gain over mid-frequency range ....

A] Changes abruptly with frequency

B] <u>Is constant</u>

C] Changes uniformly with frequency

D] None of the above

4. In obtaining the frequency response curve of an amplifier, the ....

A] Amplifier level output is kept constant

B] Amplifier frequency is held constant

C] Generator frequency is held constant

D] <u>Generator output level is held constant</u>

5. An advantage of RC coupling scheme is the ....Good impedance matching

A] Economy

B] <u>High efficiency</u>

C] None of the above

6. The best frequency response is of .... coupling

A] RC

B] Transformer

C] <u>Direct</u>

D] None of the above

7. Transformer coupling is used for .... amplification

A] _Power_
B] Voltage
C] Current
D] None of the above

8. In an RC coupling scheme, the coupling capacitor CC must be large enough ....
A] To pass d.c. between the stages
B] _Not to attenuate the low frequencies_
C] To dissipate high power
D] None of the above

9. In RC coupling, the value of coupling capacitor is about ....
A] 100 pF
B] 0.1 µF
C] 0.01 µF
D] _10 µF_

11. When a multistage amplifier is to amplify d.c. signal, then one must use .... coupling
A] RC
B] Transformer
C] _Direct_
D] None of the above

12. .... coupling provides the maximum voltage gain
A] RC
B] _Transformer_
C] Direct
D] Impedance

13. In practice, voltage gain is expressed ....
A] _In db_
B] In volts
C] As a number
D] None of the above

14. Transformer coupling provides high efficiency because ....
A] Collector voltage is stepped up
B] _resistance is low_
C] collector voltage is stepped down
D] none of the above

15. Transformer coupling is generally employed when load resistance is ....

A] Large

B] Very large

C] <u>Small</u>

D] None of the above

16. If a three-stage amplifier has individual stage gains of 10 db, 5 db and 12 db, then total gain in db is ....

A] 600 db

B] 24 db

C] 14 db

D] <u>27 db</u>

17. The final stage of a multistage amplifier uses ....

A] RC coupling

B] <u>Transformer coupling</u>

C] Direct coupling

D] Impedance coupling

18. The ear is not sensitive to ....

A] <u>Frequency distortion</u>

B] Amplitude distortion

C] Frequency as well as amplitude distortion

D] None of the above

19. RC coupling is not used to amplify extremely low frequencies because ....

A] There is considerable power loss

B] There is hum in the output

C] <u>Electrical size of coupling capacitor becomes very large</u>

D] None of the above

20. In transistor amplifiers, we use .... transformer for impedance matching

A] Step up

B] <u>Step down</u>

C] Same turn ratio

D] None of the above

21. The lower and upper cut off frequencies are also called ....
frequencies

A] Sideband

B] Resonant

C] Half-resonant

D] <u>Half-power</u>

22. A gain of 1,000,000 times in power is expressed by ....

A] 30 db

B] 60 db

C] 120 db

D] 600 db

23. A gain of 1000 times in voltage is expressed by ....

A] 60 db

B] 30 db

C] 120 db

D] 600 db

24. 1 db corresponds to .... change in power level

A] 50%

B] 35%

C] 26%

D] 22%

25. 1 db corresponds to .... change in voltage or current level

A] 40%

B] 80%

C] 20%

D] 25%

26. The frequency response of transformer coupling is ....

A] Good

B] Very good

C] Excellent

D] Poor

27. In the initial stages of a multistage amplifier, we use ....

A] RC coupling

B] Transformer coupling

C] Direct coupling

D] None of the above

28. The total gain of a multistage amplifier is less than the product of the gains of individual stages due to ....

A] Power loss in the coupling device

B] Loading effect of the next stage

C] The use of many transistors

D] The use of many capacitors

29. The gain of an amplifier is expressed in db because ....

A] It is a simple unit

B] Calculations become easy

C] Human ear response is logarithmic

D] None of the above

30. If the power level of an amplifier reduces to half, the db gain will fall by ....

A] 5 db

B] 2 db

C] 10 db

D] 3 db

31. A current amplification of 2000 is a gain of ....

A] 3 db

B] 66 db

C] 20 db

D] 200 db

32. An amplifier receives 0.1 W of input signal and delivers 15 W of signal power. What is the power gain in db?

A] 8 db

B] 6 db

C] 5 db

D] 4 db

33. The power output of an audio system is 18 W. For a person to notice an increase in the output (loudness or sound intensity) of the system, what must the output power be increased to ?

A] 2 W

B] 6 W

C] 68 W

D] None of the above

34. The output of a microphone is rated at -52 db. The reference level is 1V under specified conditions. What is the output voltage of this microphone under the same sound conditions?

A] 5 mV

B] 2 mV

C] 8 mV

D] 5 mV

35. RC coupling is generally confined to low power applications because of ....

A] Large value of coupling capacitor

B] Low efficiency

C] Large number of components

D] None of the above

36. The number of stages that can be directly coupled is limited because ....

A] <u>Changes in temperature cause thermal instability</u>

B] Circuit becomes heavy and costly

C] It becomes difficult to bias the circuit

D] None of the above

37. The purpose of RC or transformer coupling is to ....

A] Block a.c.

B] <u>Separate bias of one stage from another</u>

C] Increase thermal stability

D] None of the above

38. The upper or lower cut off frequency is also called ....frequency

A] Resonant

B] Sideband

C] <u>3 db</u>

D] None of the above

39. The bandwidth of a single stage amplifier is .... that of a multistage amplifier

A] <u>More than</u>

B] The same as

C] Less than

D] Data insufficient

40. The value of emitter capacitor CE in a multistage amplifier is about ....

A] 1 μF

B] 100 pF

C] 0.01 μF

D] <u>50 μF</u>

1. A semiconductor is formed by .... bonds.

A] <u>Covalent</u>

B] Electrovalent

C] Co-ordinate

D] None of the above

2. A semiconductor has .... temperature coefficient of resistance.

A] Positive

B] Zero

C] <u>Negative</u>

D] None of the above

3. The most commonly used semiconductor is ....

A] Germanium

B] <u>Silicon</u>

C] Carbon

D] Sulphur

6. The resistivity of a pure silicon is about ....

A] 100 O cm

B] <u>6000 O cm</u>

C] 3 x 105 O m

D] 6 x 10-8 O cm

7. When a pure semiconductor is heated, its resistance ....

A] Goes up

B] <u>Goes down</u>

C] Remains the same

D] Can't say

8. The strength of a semiconductor crystal comes from ....

A] Forces between nuclei

B] Forces between protons

C] <u>Electron-pair bonds</u>

D] None of the above

9. When a pentavalent impurity is added to a pure semiconductor, it becomes ....

A] An insulator

B] An intrinsic semiconductor

C] p-type semiconductor

D] <u>n-type semiconductor</u>

10. Addition of pentavalent impurity to a semiconductor createsmany ....

A] <u>Free electrons</u>

B] Holes

C] Valence electrons

D] Bound electrons

11. A pentavalent impurity has .... Valence electrons

A] 35

B] <u>4</u>

C] 6

12. An n-type semiconductor is ....

A] Positively charged

B] Negatively charged

C] <u>Electrically neutral</u>

D] None of the above

14. Addition of trivalent impurity to a semiconductor creates many ....

A] <u>Holes</u>

B] Free electrons

C] Valence electrons

D] Bound electrons

15. A hole in a semiconductor is defined as ....

A] A free electron

B] <u>The incomplete part of an electron pair bond</u>

C] A free proton

D] A free neutron

16. The impurity level in an extrinsic semiconductor is about ..... of pure semiconductor.

A] 10 atoms for 108 atoms

B] <u>1 atom for 108 atoms</u>

C] 1 atom for 104 atoms

D] 1 atom for 100 atoms

17. As the doping to a pure semiconductor increases, the bulk resistance of the semiconductor ....

A] Remains the same

B] Increases

C] <u>Decreases</u>

D] None of the above

18. A hole and electron in close proximity would tend to ....

A] Repel each other

B] <u>Attract each other</u>

C] Have no effect on each other

D] None of the above

19. In a semiconductor, current conduction is due to ....

A] Only holes

B] Only free electrons

C] <u>Holes and free electrons</u>

D] None of the above

20. The random motion of holes and free electrons due to thermal agitation is called ....

A] <u>Diffusion</u>

B] Pressure

C] Ionisation

D] None of the above

21. A forward biased pn junction diode has a resistance of the order of

A] <u>Ok</u>

B] O

C] MO

D] None of the above

22. The battery connections required to forward bias a pn junction are ......

A] <u>+ve terminal to p and −ve terminal to n</u>

B] -ve terminal to p and +ve terminal to n

C] -ve terminal to p and −ve terminal to n

D] None of the above

23. The barrier voltage at a pn junction for germanium is about ....

A] 5 V

B] 3 V

C] Zero

D] <u>3 V</u>

24. In the depletion region of a pn junction, there is a shortage of ....

A] Acceptor ions

B] <u>Holes and electrons</u>

C] Donor ions

D] None of the above

25. A reverse bias pn junction has ....

A] narrow depletion layer

B] <u>Almost no current</u>

C] Very low resistance

D] Large current flow

26. A pn junction acts as a ....

A] Controlled switch

B] Bidirectional switch

C] <u>Unidirectional switch</u>

D] None of the above

27. A reverse biased pn junction has resistance of the order of

A] Ok

B] O

C] MO

D] None of the above

28. The leakage current across a pn junction is due to ....

A] Minority carriers

B] Majority carriers

C] Junction capacitance

D] None of the above

29. When the temperature of an extrinsic semiconductor is increased, the pronounced effect is on......

A] Junction capacitance

B] Minority carriers

C] Majority carriers

D] None of the above

30. With forward bias to a pn junction , the width of depletion layer ....

A] Decreases

B] Increases

C] Remains the same

D] None of the above

31. The leakage current in a pn junction is of the order of

A] Aa

B] mA

C] kA

D] μA

32. In an intrinsic semiconductor, the number of free electrons ....

A] Equals the number of holes

B] Is greater than the number of holes

C] Is less than the number of holes

D] None of the above

33. At room temperature, an intrinsic semiconductor has ....

A] Many holes only

B] A few free electrons and holes

C] Many free electrons only

D] No holes or free electrons

34. At absolute temperature, an intrinsic semiconductor has ....

A] A few free electrons

B] Many holes

C] Many free electrons

D] <u>No holes or free electrons</u>

35. At room temperature, an intrinsic silicon crystal acts approximately as ......

A] A battery

B] A conductor

C] <u>An insulator</u>

D] A piece of copper wire

1.In which of the following base systems is 123 not a valid number?

(a) Base 10

(b) Base 16

(c)Base8

(d) <u>Base 3</u>

2. Storage of 1 KB means the following number of bytes

(a) 1000

(b)964

(c)<u>1024</u>

(d) 1064

3. What is the octal equivalent of the binary number:

10111101

(a)675

(b)<u>275</u>

(c) 572

(d) 573.

4. Pick out the CORRECT statement:

(a) In a positional number system, each symbol represents the same value irrespective of its position

(b) The highest symbol in a position number system as a value equal to the number of symbols in the system

(c) <u>It is not always possible to find the exact binary</u>

(d) Each hexadecimal digit can be represented as a sequence of three binary symbols.

5.The binary code of (21.125)10 is

(a) <u>10101.001</u>

(b) 10100.001

(c) 10101.010

(d) 10100.111.

6.A NAND gate is called a universal logic element because

(a) it is used by everybody

(b) <u>any logic function can be realized by NAND gates alone</u>

(c) all the minization techniques are applicable for optimum NAND gate realization

(d) many digital computers use NAND gates.

7. Digital computers are more widely used as compared to analog computers,

because they are

(a) less expensive

(b) always more accurate and faster

(c) <u>useful over wider ranges of problem types</u>

(d) easier to maintain.

8. Most of the digital computers do not have floating point hardware because

(a) <u>floating point hardware is costly</u>

(b) it is slower than software

(c) it is not possible to perform floating point addition by hardware

(d) of no specific reason.

9. The number 1000 would appear just immediately after

(a) FFFF (hex)

(b) 1111 (binary)

(c) 7777 (octal)

(d) <u>All of the above.</u>

10. (1(10101)2 is

(a) <u>(37)10</u>

(b) (69)10

(c) (41)10

(d) — (5)10

11. The number of Boolean functions that can be generated by n variables is equal to

(a) 2n

(b) <u>22 n</u>

(c) 2n-1

(d) — 2n

12. Consider the representation of six-bit numbers by two's complement, one's complement, or by sign and magnitude: In which representation is there overflow from the addition of the integers 011000 and 011000?

(a) Two's complement only

(b) Sign and magnitude and one's complement only

(c) Two's complement and one's complement only

(d) All three representations.

13. A hexadecimal odometer displays F 52 F. The next reading will be

(a)F52E

(b)G52F

(c)F53F

(d)F53O.

14. Positive logic in a logic circuit is one in which

(a) logic 0 and 1 are represented by 0 and positive voltage respectively

(b) logic 0 and, -1 are represented by negative and positive voltages respectively

(c) logic 0 voltage level is higher than logic 1 voltage level

(d) logic 0 voltage level is lower than logic 1 voltage level.

15. Which of the following gate is a two-level logic gate

(a) OR gate

(b) NAND gate

(c) EXCLUSIVE OR gate

(d) NOT gate.

16. Among the logic families, the family which can be used at very high frequency greater than 100 MHz in a 4 bit synchronous counter is

(a) TTLAS

(b) CMOS

(c)ECL

(d)TTLLS

17. An AND gate will function as OR if

(a) all the inputs to the gates are "1"

(b) all the inputs are '0'

(c) either of the inputs is "1"

(d) all the inputs and outputs are complemented.

18. An OR gate has 6 inputs. The number of input words in its truth table are

(a)6

(b)32

(c) 64

(d) 128

19. A debouncing circuit is

(a) an astable MV

(b) a bistable MV

(c) <u>a latch</u>

(d) a monostable MV.

20. NAND. gates are preferred over others because these

(a) have lower fabrication area

(b) <u>can be used to make any gate</u>

(c) consume least electronic power

(d) provide maximum density in a chip.

21. In case of OR gate, no matter what the number of inputs, a

(a) <u>1 at any input causes the output to be at logic 1</u>

(b) 1 at any input causes the output to be at logic 0

(c) 0 any input causes the output to be at logic 0

(d) 0 at any input causes the output to be at logic 1.

22. The fan put of a 7400 NAND gate is

(a)2TTL

(b)5TTL

(c)8TTL

(d)<u>10TTL</u>

23. Excess-3 code is known as

(a) Weighted code

(b) Cyclic redundancy code

(c) <u>Self-complementing code</u>

(d) Algebraic code.

k24. Assuming 8 bits for data, 1 bit for parity, I start bit and 2 stop bits, the number of characters that 1200 BPS communication line can transmit is

(a)10 CPS

(b)120 CPS

(c) <u>12CPS</u>

(d) None of the above.

1. "The mass of an ion liberated at an electrode is directly proportional to the quantity of electricity".

The above statement is associated with

(a) Newton's law

(b) Faraday's law of electromagnetic

(c) <u>Faraday's law of electrolysis</u>

(d) Gauss's law

2. The charge required to liberate one gram equivalent of any substance is known as _______ constant

(a) time

(b) <u>Faraday's</u>

(c) Boltzman

3. During the charging of a lead-acid cell

(a) <u>its voltage increases</u>

(b) it gives out energy

(c) its cathode becomes dark chocolate brown in colour

(d) specific gravity of H_2SO_4 decreases

4. The capacity of a lead-acid cell does not depend on its

(a) temperature

(b) <u>rate of charge</u>

(c) rate of discharge

(d) quantity of active material

5. During charging the specific gravity of the electrolyte of a lead-acid battery

(a) <u>increases</u>

(b) decreases

(c) remains the same

(d) becomes zero

6. The active materials on the positive and negative plates of a fully charged leadacid battery are

(a) lead and lead peroxide

(b) lead sulphate and lead

(c) <u>lead peroxide and lead</u>

(d) none of the above

7. When a lead-acid battery is in fully charged condition, the colour of its positive

plate is

(a) dark grey

(b) brown

(c) <u>dark brown</u>

(d) none of above

8. The active materials of a nickel-iron battery are

(a) nickel hydroxide

(6) powdered iron and its oxide

(c) 21% solution of KOH

(d) <u>all of the above</u>

9. The ratio of ampere-hour efficiency to watt-hour efficiency of a lead-acid cell is

(a) just one

(b) <u>always greater than one</u>

(c) always less than one

(d) none of the above.

10. The best indication about the state of charge on a lead-acid battery is given by

(a) output voltage

(b) temperature of electrolyte

(c) <u>specific gravity of electrolyte</u>

(d) none of the above

11. The storage battery generally used in electric power station is

(a) nickel-cadmium battery

(b) zinc-carbon battery

(c) <u>lead-acid battery</u>

(d) none of the above

12. The output voltage of a charger is

(a) less than the battery voltage

(b) <u>higher than the battery voltage</u>

(c) the same as the battery voltage

(d) none of the above

13. Cells are connected in series in order to

(a) <u>increase the voltage rating</u>

(6) increase the current rating

(c) increase the life of the cells

(d) none of the above

14. Five 2 V cells are connected in parallel. The output voltage is

(a) 1 V

(6) 1.5 V

(c) 1.75 V

(d) <u>2 V</u>

15. The capacity of a battery is expressed in terms of

(a) current rating

(b) voltage rating

(c) <u>ampere-hour rating</u>

(d) none of the above

16. Duringthe charging and discharging of a nickel-iron cell

(a) corrosive fumes are produced

(b) <u>water is neither formed nor absorbed</u>

(c) nickel hydroxide remains unsplit

(d) its e.m.f. remains constant

17. As compared to constant-current system, the constant-voltage system of charging a lead acid cell has the advantage of

(a) reducing time of charging

(b) increasing cell capacity

(c) <u>both (a) and (b)</u>

(d) avoiding excessive gassing

18. A dead storage battery can be revived by

(a) adding distilled water

(6) adding so-called battery restorer

(c) a dose of H2SO4

(d) <u>none of the above</u>

19. As compared to a lead-acid cell, the efficiency of a nickel-iron cell is less due to its

(a) compactness

(b) lower e.m.f.

(c) small quantity of electrolyte used

(d) <u>higher internal resistance</u>

20. Trickle charging of a storage battery helps to

(a) maintain proper electrolyte level

(b) increase its reserve capacity

(c) prevent sulphation

(d) <u>keep it fresh and fully charged</u>

21. Those substances of the cell which take active part in chemical combination and hence produce electricity during charging or discharging are known as_______materials.

(a) passive

(b) <u>active</u>

(c) redundant

(d) inert

22. In a lead-acid cell dilute sulphuric acid (electrolyte) approximately comprises the following

(a) one part H2O, three parts H2SO4

(b) two parts H2O, two parts H2SO4

(c) <u>three parts H2O, one part H2SO4</u>

(d) all H2S04

23. It is noticed that durum charging

(a) there is a rise in voltage

(b) energy is absorbed by the cell

(c) specific gravity of H2SO4 is increased

(d) <u>all of the above</u>

24. It is noticed that during discharging the following does not happen

(a) both anode and cathode become PbS04

(b) specific gravity of H2SO4 decreases

(c) voltage of the cell decreases

(d) <u>the cell absorbs energy</u>

25. The ampere-hour efficiency of a leadacid cell is normally between

(a) 20 to 30%

(b) 40 to 50%

(c) 60 to 70%

(d) <u>90 to 95%</u>

26. The watt-hour efficiency of a lead-acid cell varies between

(a) 25 to 35%

(b) 40 to 60%

(c) <u>70 to 80%</u>

(d) 90 to 95%

27. The capacity of a lead-acid cell is measured in

(a) amperes

(b) <u>ampere-hours</u>

(c) watts

(d) watt-hours

28. The capacity of a lead-acid cell depends on

(a) rate of discharge

(b) temperature

(c) density of electrolyte

(d) <u>all above</u>

29. When the lead-acid cell is fully charged, the electrolyte assumes ______appearance

(a) dull

(b) reddish

(c) bright

(d) <u>milky</u>

30. The e.m.f. of an Edison cell, when fully charged, is nearly
(a) 1.4 V
(b) 1 V
(c) 0.9 V
(d) 0.8 V

31. The internal resistance of an alkali cell is nearly ______ times that of the leadacid cell.
(a) two
(b) three
(c) four
(d) five

32. The average charging voltage for alkali cell is about
(a) 1 V
(b) 1.2 V
(c) 1.7 V
(d) 2.1 V

33. On the average the ampere-hour efficiency of an Edison cell is about
(a) 40%
(b) 60%
(c) 70%
(d) 80%

34. The active material of the positive plates of silver-zinc batteries is
(a) silver oxide
(b) lead oxide
(c) lead
(d) zinc powder

35. Lead-acid cell has a life of nearly charges and discharges
(a) 500
(b) 700
(c) 1000
(d) 1250

36. Life of the Edison cell is at least
(a) five years
(b) seven years
(c) eight years
(d) ten years

37. The internal resistance of a lead-acid cell is that of Edison cell
(a) less than

(b) more than

(c) equal to

(d) none of the above

38. Electrolyte used in an Edison cell is

(a) NaOH

(b) <u>KOH</u>

(c) HC1

(d) HN03

39. Electrolyte used in a lead-acid cell is

(a) NaOH

(b) onlyH2S04

(c) only water

(d) <u>dilute H2SO4</u>

40. Negative plate of an Edison cell is made of

(a) copper

(b) lead

(c) <u>iron</u>

(d) silver oxide

41. The open circuit voltage of any storage cell depends wholly upon

(a) its chemical constituents

(b) on the strength of its electrolyte

(c) its temperature

(d) <u>all above</u>

42. The specific gravity of electrolyte is measured by

(a) manometer

(6) a mechanical gauge

(c) <u>hydrometer</u>

(d) psychrometer

43. When the specific gravity of the electrolyte of a lead-acid cell is reduced to 1.1 to 1.15 the cell is in

(a) charged state

(b) <u>discharged state</u>

(c) both (a) and (b)

(d) active state

44. In _______ system the charging current is intermittently controlled at either a

maximum or minimum value

(a) <u>two rate charge control</u>

(b) trickle charge

(c) floating charge

(d) an equalizing charge

45. Over charging

(a) produces excessive gassing

(b) loosens the active material

(e) increases the temperature resulting in buckling of plates

(d) <u>all above</u>

46. Undercharging

(a) <u>reduces specific gravity of the electrolyte</u>

(b) increases specific gravity of the electrolyte

(c) produces excessive gassing

(d) increases the temperature

47. Internal short circuits are caused by

(a) breakdown of one or more separators

(b) excess accumulation of sediment at the bottom of the cell

(c) <u>both (a) and (b)</u>

(d) none of the above

48. The effect of sulphation is that the internal resistance

(a) <u>increases</u>

(b) decreases

(c) remains same

(d) none of the above

49. Excessive formation of lead sulphate on the surface of the plates happens because of

(a) allowing a battery to stand in discharged condition for a long time

(b) topping up with electrolyte

(c) persistent undercharging

(d) <u>all above</u>

50. The substances which combine together to store electrical energy during the charge are called _______ materials

(a) <u>active</u>

(b) passive

(c) inert

(d) dielectric

Q.1. Which of the following is the biggest unit of memory?

A] <u>Gigabytes.</u>

B] bytes.

C] Megabytes.

D] Kilobytes.

Q.2. The primary purpose of software is to turn data into.

A] Website.

B] <u>Infromation.</u>

C] Programs.

D] Objects.

Q.3. GUI Stands for

A] <u>Graphical User Interface.</u>

B] Greater User Interface.

C] Graphical Union Interface.

D] Graphical User Intereat.

Q.4. Key board keys that have arrows on them are called -

A] Function Keys.

B] <u>Navigation Keys.</u>

C] Typewriter Keys.

D] Special purpose keys.

Q.5. ASSCII, EBCDIC and Unicode are examples of Application Software's

A] True.

B<u>] False.</u>

Q.6. The easiest way to access any part of the screen in the windows operating system is using the.

A] Key Board.

B] Rat.

C] <u>Mouse.</u>

D]] Joystick.

Q.7. A software is also called as a

A] Procedure.

B] Data.

C] <u>Programs.</u>

D] Information.

Q.10. .... Utility identifies unnecessary files on the hard disk and erases them based on users command.

A] Backup.

B] File Compression.

C] Uninstall Programs.

D] <u>] Disk Clean up.</u>

Q.11. This type of software is designs to help you be more productive tasks, and is widely used in nearly every disc live and occupation.

A] Communication Software.

B] Utility Software.

C] <u>Basic Application Software.</u>

D] System Software.

Q.12. Minicomputers are also known as.

A] <u>Mid Range Computers.</u>

B] Personal Digital Computers.

C] Mainframe Computers.

D] Laptop Computers.

Q.13. Which of the following device is used to play fast games on a computers.

A] Touch Surface.

B] Touch Screen.2

C] Track Ball.

D] <u>Joystick.</u>

Q.14. Which of the following would not be considered as portable computer.

A] <u>Desktop Computer.</u>

B] Note book computer.

C] Personal Digital Assistant.

D] None of these.

Q.19............. is a pointing device.

A] <u>Mouse.</u>

B] Printer.

C] Scanner.

D] Keyboard.

Q.20. The keyboards keys that are labelled F1, F2 and so on are called ....

A] <u>Function Keys.</u>

B] Numeric Keys.

C] Typewriter Keys.

D] Special purpose keys.

Q.21. The keyboard keys like Caps lock that turn on features on or off are called.

A] Function Keys.

B] Combination Keys.

C] <u>Toggle Keys.</u>

D] Special Purpose Keys.

Q.22. Word processing, electronic spread sheets, database managers and graphics programs are all grouped under the title.

A] Browsings Programs.

B] Operating System.

C] <u>Application Software</u>.

D] Data and Information.

Q.23. Keyboard, mouse, monitor, and system unit collectively also known as

A] Solid ware.

B] Software.

C] <u>Hardware.</u>

D] Firm ware.

Q.29. The keys labelled 0-9 on the keyboard are called.

A] Function Keys.

B] <u>Numeric Keys.</u>

C] Typewriter Keys.

D] Special purpose keys.

Q.31. .... consists of step-by-step introductions that tells the computer how to complete the task.

A] <u>Programs.</u>

B] Hardware.

C] Data.

D] Objects.

Q.33.......... is a background soft ware that helps the computer to manage its internal resources.

A] <u>System Software</u>.

B] Information.

C] Objects.

D] None of these.

Q.35. Following are the file compression programs, EXCEPT

A] Win Zip.

B] <u>RAID.</u>

C] Win RAR.

D] PK Zip.

Q.38. The keyboard keys that have arrows on them are called.

A] Function Keys.

B] Combination Keys.

C] <u>Navigation Keys</u>

D] Special Purpose Keys.

Q.42.......... are graphical objects used to represent and open commonly used applications.

A] G.U.I..

B] Primers'.

C] Windows NT.

D] <u>Icons.</u>

Q.44. Data stored in RAM is

A] Is non-volatile.

B] <u>Is only there while the power is on.</u>

C] Remains only a few minutes after the power is turned off.

D] Is permanent and only lost in power failure.

Q.46. Primary function of a monitor is to display information to the user.

A] <u>True.</u>

B] False.

Q.47. Random Access Memory] RAM. is .... type of memory.

A] Permanent.

B] <u>Temporary.</u>

C] Flash.

D] Smart.

Q.5. You can click on.............. to learn how to use Windows Vista, obtain troubleshooting information, receive support and more.

A] "Search"

B] "Windows"

C] "Start"

D] <u>"Help & Support"</u>

Q.6. In MS paint to draw a curved line, we have to click the................... Icon.

A] <u>"Curve"</u>

B] "Line"

C] "Polygon"

D] "Rectangle"

Q.7. .... refers to the height and width of the characters to be printed.

A] <u>"Font Size"</u>

B] "Border"

C] "Cell"

D] "Font Style"

Q.8. There is button which is not present on the "Title bar".

A] Minimize

B] <u>Start</u>

C] Maximise

D] Close

Q.9. Disk Defragmenter is used to remove unnecessary files on your hard disk to free up space and your computer run faster.

A] True

B] <u>False</u>

Q.11. To start the calculator application click "Start" and select "All Programs Accessories Calculator."

A] <u>True</u>

B] False

Q.12. .... can be used to create and format large and complex text documents.

A] "Calculator"

B] <u>"WordPad"</u>

C] "Notepad"

D] "Text Pad"

Q.14. A folder system is also called a "................"

A] "Direction System"

B] <u>"Directory System"</u>

C] "Directory list"

D] "Folder book"

Q.17. A .... is like a container in which you can store files.

A] "Icon"

B] "document"

C] <u>"Folder"</u>

D] "Sheet"

Q.18. The operating system's job is .... to

A] Execute many useful commands easily.

B] to make request for service through a defined application programme interface.

C] <u>to control the computer at the most fundamental level.</u>

D] None of these.

Q.19. The windows interface is based on ....

A] <u>"Graphical user Interface" or GUI</u>

B] Application Programme Interface or] API.

C] "Clipboard"

D] None of these

Q.23. A file created using Notepad is stored with the extension..................

.

A] <u>".txt"</u>

B] ".docx"

C] ".png"

D] ".jpg"

Q.25. When your computer is booted and is ready to use, the screen you see is called the ....

A] "Table top"

B] <u>"Desktop"</u>

C] "Laptop"

D] None of these

Q.27. .... is designed to prevent and remove spy ware.

A] User Account Control

B] Windows Firewall

C] <u>Windows Defender</u>

D] Parental Controls

Q.29. What is "Windows Aero"

A] It is the graphical user interface for Windows XP.

B] <u>It is the graphical user interface for Windows Vista.</u>

C] Application Program

D] None of these

Q.30. Which is the basic program of a computer?

A] <u>Operating System</u>

B] Software Program

C] Application Program

D] None of these

Q.34. The .... Menu is used to enhance the appearance of the contained presented in a document.

A] "Insert"

B] "Edit" ?

C] <u>"Format"</u>

D] "File"

Q.35. The "text" tool is used to add text to a paint object.

A] <u>True</u>

B] False

Q.36. "............" helps in guarding your computer against malicious software.

A] <u>"Windows Firewall"</u>

B] "Windows Defender"

C] "Spy ware"

D] of these.

Q.37. .... is a basic text editing programme and it is most commonly used to view or edit text files.

A] "Calculator"

B] <u>"Notepad"</u>

C] "Address book"

D] "Paint"

Q.38. In a windows operating system screen saver

A] is helps in guarding your computer against many types of malicious software.

B] is a long, vertical bar that is displayed on the side of your desktop.

C] <u>is a programme that displays on image, animation, or just a blank screen on a Computer after on input has been received for a certain length of time.</u>

D] None of these.

Q.40. The programmes on the .... in Windows Vista remain there and are always available for you to click to start them.

A] the "Most frequently use programmes list.

B] <u>"pinned items list"</u>

C] "Documents"

D] "Control Panel"

Q.41. In Windows Vista .... is a power-saving state.

A] Log off

B] <u>Sleep</u>

C] Restart

D] Lock

Q.42. AERO is an abbreviation of ....

A] <u>Authentic, Energetic, Reflective and Open.</u>

B] Essential, Reflective and Open.

C] Arithmetic, Essential, Reflective and Object.

D] Authentic, Essential, Reflective and Open.

Q.43. At the bottom of the screen, you can see a long, thin bar which is called as ....

A] <u>"Task bar"</u>

B] "Title bar"

C] "Menu bar"

D] "Spacebar"

Q.44. In Windows Vista a "Clipboard" is ....

A] an application program

B] <u>a temporary storage area for information that you have copied or moved from one place and plan to use somewhere else.</u>

C] an operating system.

D] None of these.

Q.45. .... is a basic text editing programme and it is most commonly used to view or edit text files.

A] "Calculator"

B] <u>"Notepad"</u>

C] "Address book"

D] "Paint"

Q.46. ...., is a drawing programme that can be used to create modify graphic images.

A] "Brush"

B] <u>"Paint"</u>

C] "Notepad"

D] "WordPad"

Q.47. The .... menu is used to enhance the apperance of the content presented in a document.

A] "Insert"

B] "Edit"

C] <u>"Format"</u>

D] "File"

Q.48. A .... is a rectangular section on the screen that is used to display information and other programme.

A] Icon

B] Desktop

C] <u>Window</u>

D] Panel

Q.51. The name of a file consist of two parts

A] Folder Name

B] use Extension

C] <u>File Name</u>

D] use Sub folder Name

Q.52. We can navigate through text using

A] Cpu

B] <u>Mouse</u>

C] Key board

D] Monitor

Q.1. In MS Word 2007 when text is selected, a "............" is automatically displayed.

A] Taskbar

B] Main Toolbar

C] <u>Mini Toolbar</u>

D] Menu bar

Q.2. You can make for a TOC using:

A] Heading styles.

B] Custom styles.

C] Outline levels.

D] <u>All of these.</u>

Q.3. .... contains command for opening, saving, printing and closing a file.

A] "Home"

B] <u>"Office Button"</u>

C] "View"

D] "Insert"

Q.4. .... offers a wide variety of options to design documents.

A] Microsoft Excel

B] Microsoft PowerPoint

C] <u>Microsoft Word</u>

D] Microsoft Access

Q.5. All of the following Ribbon tabs are displayed in Word 2007, EXCEPT

A] Home

B] Insert

C] <u>Tools</u>

D] Page Layout

Q.9. In Word, a file is called as a ....

A] "template"

B] "form"

C] "database"

D] <u>"Document"</u>

Q.13. A .... is a reference from one part of a document to related information in same another part.

A] Hyperlink

B] <u>Cross-reference</u>

C] Document

D] Linkage

Q.14. For Indentation you may use the "Decrease Indent" and "Increase Indent" icons in the "Paragraph" group on the "............." tab for indenting your text.

A] Insert

B] <u>Home</u>

C] Page Layout

D] Data

Q.16. The "..............." is a dictionary of synonyms which you can use to find words that are synonyms with a term.

A] Translate

B] Spelling

C] <u>Thesaurus</u>

D] Research

Q.17. A " .... " is a listing of the topics that appear in a document with their associated page references.

A] Index

B] Table

C] Clipboard

D] <u>Table of contents</u>

Q.18. You can format your document automatically applying styles, available in MS Word 2007.

A] <u>True</u>

B] False

Q.19. A "............." is a connection to a location in the current document to another document or Web Site.

A] Link

B] <u>hyperlink</u>

C] hypolink

D] linkage

Q.26. A "................." is a pre-designed document useful for creating common purpose documents such as a fax, invoice or business letter.

A] <u>Template</u>

B] File

C] Form

D] Database

Q.28. A "............." is used to organize information into an easy-to-read format of horizontal rows and vertical columns.

A] Cell

B] Sheet

C] Box

D] <u>Table</u>

Q.29. To remove individual character at the left you may press "............".

A] Delete

B] <u>Backspace</u>

C] Enter

D] Spacebar

Q.30. When you click on "Format Printer" icon on the "Home" tab, you can see that your mouse pointer changes to a "............." icon.

A] <u>paintbrush</u>

B] I-beam

C] Arrow

D] 4-Way arrow

Q.33. When you move your mouse over a button, a .... is displayed. That provides a detailed description of what the button does.

A] <u>Super-tooltip</u>

B] Sub-tooltip

C] Info

D] Key-tip

Q.35. .... Applications help you to create different types of written documents such as personal letters, from letters, brochures, faxes and even professional manuals.

A] <u>Word Processor</u>

B] Word Pad

C] Note Pad

D] None of these

Q.40. To automatically correct the document, we use

A] <u>The auto correct feature</u>

B] The auto complete feature

C] Formatting

D] Building Blocks

Q.41. A "................" is a common application for news paper columns.

A] News reading

B] <u>News letter</u>

C] News

D] News editor

Q.47. A "..............." is used to mark a certain location in a document.

A] Index

B] Hyperlink

C] <u>Bookmark</u>

D] Table

Q.50. While changing the level of an item in hierarchy you can increase the indent by using

A] <u>"Tab"</u>

B] "Backspace"

C] "Delete"

D] "Spacebar"

Q.51. Footnotes or Endnotes are used to provide certain "........................".

A] <u>References</u>

B] Information

C] Points

D] Lists

Q.1. In formula bar, an adjacent range is specified by giving the starting and editing cell addresses separated by a

A] Semicolon

B] Comma

C] Full stop

D] <u>Colon</u>

Q.3. A .... is a visual representation of data and conveys the information in an easy to understand and attractive manner.

A] <u>chart</u>

B] table

C] picture

D] graphic

Q.4. In formulas, a non-adjacent range is specified by giving the cell addresses separated by a ....

A] Semicolon

B] <u>Comma</u>

C] Full stop

D] Colon

Q.5. You can use the .... to enter and edit data, instead of editing directly in your work sheet.

A] <u>formula bar</u>

B] title bar

C] menu bar

D] space bar

Q.6. Your Excel 2007 file is stored with the extension "............".

A] ".docx"

B] <u>".xlsx"</u>

C] ".xltx"

D] ".zltx"

Q.9. The "............" tab contains proofing tools like spell check.

A] <u>"Review"</u>

B] "Data"

C] "View"

D] "Insert"

Q.18. "............." is a method which aids you in forecasting values.

A] "Find"

B] "Replace"

C] <u>"Goal Seek"</u>

D] "Go to"

Q.20. A "..............." is a prewritten formula the performs calculations automatically.

A] <u>"Function"</u>

B] "Equation"

C] "Template"

D] "Reaction"

Q.21. MS Excel 2007 is used for different types of .... varying from vary simple to complex.

A] <u>calculations</u>

B] manipulations

C] presentations

D] expressions

Q.25. While changing the level of an item in the hierarchy you can increase the indent by using.

A] "Tab"

B] "Backspace"

C] "Delete"

D] "Spacebar"

Q.26. To set margins, select "Margins" from the "Page Setup" group on the "Page Layout" tab.

A] True

B] False

Q.27. To remove individual character at the left you may press "..............".

A] Delete

B] Backspace

C] Enter

D] Spacebar

Q.28. Drop caps are the first character/s at the beginning that are enlarged, conversing several lines.

A] True

B] False

Q.29. The intersection of a row and a column is called a "...............".

A] Table

B] Cell

C] Data

D] Sheet

Q.30. A .... is a file that is provided by the application in a "ready to use" format.

A] Sheet

B] Template

C] Book

D] Report

Q.31. A .... is a visual representation of data and conveys the information in a easy to understand and attractive manner.

A] Chart

B] Table

C] Picture

D] Graphic

Q.35. "............" are individual designs that can be applied to different parts to the document.

A] "Graphics"
B] "Styles"
C] "Pictures"
D] "Themes"

Q.36. "............" contains commands for opening, saving, printing, and closing a file.

A] "View" tab
B] "Office Button"
C] "Insert" tab
D] "Review" tab

Q.39. The text that appears in the top margin of the page is called the ....

A] Footer
B] Column
C] Header
D] Paragraph

Q.42. To stop the automatic relative cell references, i.e. to make the cell reference absolute, type a .... character before the column and row number.

A] # hash.
B] $ dollar.
C] % percent.
D] * star.

Q.49. In Microsoft Excel 2007, a single file or document is called a "............".

A] Workbook
B] Worksheet
C] Sheet
D] Notebook

Q.51. With the .... option, you can freeze either or both, rows and columns ie. regardless of where you are in the worksheet you can see the information in these rows and/or columns at all times.

A] Split
B] Arrange
C] Fitter
D] Freeze Panes

Q.54. A template file in MS Excel 2007 has an extension "...............".
A] .docx

B] .yltx

C] .xltx

D] .zltx

Q.55. A "............." is like an accountant's ledger consisting of rows and columns.

A] Table

B] Microsoft Excel 2007

C] Format

D] Sheet

Q.3. A "................" graphic is a visual representation of your information and ideas.

A] "WordArt"

B] "ClipArt"

C] "SmartArt"

D] "Autoshape"

Q.5. "................" refer to a ready-to-use picture.

A] "WordArt"

B] "ClipArt"

C] "SmartArt"

D] "Autoshape"

Q.8. The "............." tab contains tools that controls how to slide show is presented.

A] "Design"

B] "Slide Show"

C] "Review"

D] "View"

Q.10. .... which displays icon that represent commonly used commands such as Save, Undo, and Redo.

A] Home Button

B] The Ribbon

C] The Quick Access Tool bar

D] The Office Button

Q.11. A "..........." is a connection to a location in the current documnet, another document or a website.

A] Highlink

B] hipolink

C] linkage

D] hyperlink

Q.12. .... are used to create slide shows on the computer

A] <u>Presentation graphics</u>

B] Analytical development programs

C] Super Slide packages

D] Slide maker tools

Q.15. In graphic presentation, programmes each presentation is divided into ....

A] charts

B] <u>slides</u>

C] tables

D] pictures

Q.19. A "..............." is a pre-designed presentation designed for common purpose such as photo album or a quiz show.

A] "Chart"

B] "Table"

C] "Slide"

D] <u>"Template"</u>

Q.22. When you move your mouse over a sizing handle the pointer becomes a "..............".

A] Round Arrow

B] <u>Two-headed Arrow</u>

C] Plus Sign

D] Four-headed Arrow

Q.23. PowerPoint Presentation is a component of following application software.

A] Leap Office

B] Start Office

C] Open Office

D] <u>MS Office</u>

Q.29. You may change the presentation views by checking on the buttons displayed on the "............" at the bottom of the screen.

A] "Title bar"

B] "Menu bar"

C] "Tool bar"

D] <u>"Status bar"</u>

Q.33. In Presentation Graphics "............" are used to add information such as slide numbers, the time and date, a company logo or the presentation title to the top of a handout or notes page in your presentation, or a bottom of a slide, handout or notes.

A] Hyperlinks

B] Tables

C] Header and Footers

D] Charts

Q.35. "..............." takes up the full computer screen, like an actual slide show presentation.

A] Slide Sorter View

B] Normal View

C] Slide Show View

D] Notes Page

Q.38. If you have a large number of slides in your presentation, you may find it more convenient to use the .... to view all your slides and change their positions.

A] Normal View

B] Slide Sorter View

C] Slide Show View

D] Notes Page

Q.40. In Microsoft PowerPoint your file is stored with the .... extension.

A] psd

B] .rtf

C] .pptx

D] .docx

Q.41. When the pointer becomes a ...., you can drag placeholder to the location you wish.

A] Round arrow

B] Two-round arrow

C] Plus sign

D] Four-headed arrow

Q.43. "............." are details about a file that help identify it.

A] Desktop Properties

B] Window Properties

C] Advanced Properties

D] Document Properties

Q.46. "..............." is the main editing view.

A] Slide Sorter View

B] Normal View

C] Slide Show View

D] Notes Page

Q.49. The "..........." tab contains the basic formatting tools.

A] "Design"

B] "View"

C] "Insert"

D] "Home"

Q.2. "............." is a database object that is mainly used to enter and display records and make changes to existing records on screens.

A] query.

B] form.

C] report.

D] table.

Q.7. "............." is an electronic database management system which can store, organize access, manipulate, and present information in many different ways.

A] MS Access 2007.

B] MS Word.

C] MS Excel.

D] MS PowerPoint.

Q.11. "............." data type is used to store numbers only.

A] Auto Number.

B] Text.

C] Number.

D] Date/Time.

Q.13. "............" stores the information in Access 2007.

A] Table.

B] Queries.

C] Reports.

D] Forms.

Q.15. "..........." data type is used to store images, documents, graphs etc.

A] Hyperlink.

B] OEL Object.

C] Text.

D] Description.

Q.16. "..........." decides the maximum number of characters that can be entered in the field.

A] Format.

B] Input Mask.

C] Caption.

D] <u>Field Size.</u>

Q.17. The information in a database is stored in a ....

A] Chart.

B] Box.

C] Folder.

D] <u>Table</u>.

Q.18. "............" is the default data type and is used to store text entries like words, combinations of words and numbers and numbers that are not used in calculations.

A] Text.

B] Number.

C] Memo.

D] <u>Currency.</u>

Q.21. In Access, every database is stored in a single file which has the extension.

A] ".docx"

B] ".rtf"

C] <u>".accdb"</u>

D] ".txt"

Q.23. A .... is used to identify the data stored in a field.

A] Table.

B] <u>Field Name.</u>

C] Box.

D] Bracket.

Q.25. "..........." simplifies data entry and controls what data is required and how it is to be displayed.

A] Format.

B] <u>Input Mask.</u>

C] Caption.

D] Field Size.

Q.27. .... provides a number of data types.

A] Word 2007.

B] <u>Access 2007</u>.

C] Excel 2007.

D] PowerPoint 2007.

Q.33."............" are windows that you create and arrange in order to easily view or change the information in a table.

A] Table.

B] <u>Queries.</u>

C] Report.

D] Forms.

Q.34. "............" restricts the data easy to meet certain conditions or requirements.

A] Validation Text.

B] Default Value.

C] <u>Validation Rule.</u>

D] Format.

Q.36. "............" data type is used to store text that is too long to be stored in a text field.

A] Text.

B] Number.

C] <u>Memo.</u>

D] Currency.

Q.38. "............." specifies a field caption or a prompt for the user to enter data.

A] Format.

B] Input Mask.

C] <u>Caption.</u>

D] Field Size.

Q.43. A primary key must be

A] Unique But Permit Null.

B] <u>Unique and Not Null.</u>

C] Non-unique And Not Null.

D] Non-unique And Permit Null.

Q.44. which of the following are functions performed by a DBA?

A] Database Design.

B] System Security.

C] Backup and Recovery.

D] <u>All of the above.</u>

Q.45. "............" is a relation database management application that is used to create and analyze a database.

A] Word 2007.

B] <u>Access 2007.</u>

C] System Security.

D] PowerPoint 2007.

Q.47. A "............" is a field or set of fields in your table that provide Access with a unique identifier for every record.

A] Password.

B] Special Code.

C] <u>Primary Key.</u>

D] Unique Code.

Q.51. what is the first step of defining a database.

A] Designing the database.

B] Collection of data.

C] <u>Planning your database.</u>

D] Digitizing your data.

Q.54. DBMS means...................

A] <u>Database Management System.</u>

B] Domain Management System.

C] Domain Manangeemt Server.

D] Domain Management Style.

Q.58 You can enter up to charactess in a text field.

A] 375

B] 125

C] 235

D] <u>255</u>

Q.1. Netscape Navigator is a type of ....

A] Utility Program.

B] Operating System.

C] <u>Browser.</u>

D] Web Authoring Program.

Q.2. When you type an address such as "http://www.mkcl.org", in this .org indicates.

A] <u>Original Web Site.</u>

B] Commercial Web Site.

C] Organizational Web Site.

D] Educational Web Site.

Q.3. You can search the World Wide Web for a specific topic by using .... and.................

A] Gophers, Fido's.

B] Scanner, Search Engine.

C] <u>Search Engines, Indexes.</u>

D Browsers, Larkers.

Q.4. A] n. .... is a set of rules for how information and messages are sent over the internet.

A] <u>Protocol.</u>

B] ISP.

C] Applet.

D] HTML Hyper Text Markup Language.

Q.5. Discussion on the internet about specific topic is known as

A] News.

B] <u>News group.</u>

C] Veronica.

D] Telnet.

Q.6. Which of the following is not a type of protocol?

A] TCI/IP

B] <u>ASCII</u>

C] None of these.

D] ppp

Q.7. Which of the following is a type of protocol?

A] ASCII

B] RAM

C] <u>TCI/IP</u>

D] DBA

Q.8. The three parts of an e-mail message are

A] TCP/IP, Domain and ISP.

B] Destination, Device and Sender.

C] <u>Header, Message and Signature.</u>

D] TCP, IP and Message.

Q.9. The network connecting several computers all over the world is?

A] Intranet.

B] <u>Internet.</u>

C] Arpanet.

D] Network.

Q.10. Which of the following is a browser.

A] Web site.

B] Microsoft.

C] <u>Internet Explorer.</u>

D] www.

Q.11. The terms DNS stands for.

A] Data Naming System.

B] Do Name System.

C] <u>Domain Name System.</u>

D] Duplicate Name System.

Q.12. Internet e-mail address is .... for every user.

A] <u>Unique.</u>

B] Same.

C] Common.

D] None of these.

Q.13. For navigating any website, user has to enter

A] <u>URL.</u>

B] www.

C] PPP.

D] None of these.

Q.14. What is the full form of E-Commerce ?

A] English Commerce.

B] <u>Electronic Commerce.</u>

C] Electric Commerce.

D] Element Commerce.

Q.15. To send e-mail to someone you need ....

A] Resident Address.

B] <u>Internet Connectivity.</u>

C] Fax Address.

D] None of these.

Q.16. .... is used to see the web page.

A] Inbox.

B] Recycle bin.

C] <u>Internet Explorer.</u>

D] Network Neighbourhood.

Q.17. Full form of URL

A] Universal Resource Locator.

B] <u>Uniform Resource Locator.</u>

C] Uni Resource Locator.

D] None of these.

Q.19. Which of the following is a search engine.

A] Google.

B] Alta Vista.

C] Yahoo.

D] <u>All of these.</u>

Q.20. What is meant by E-Commerce?

A] <u>Online selling, purchasing, account handling etc.</u>

B] Subject commerce stream.

C] Electronic equipment to deal with commercial problem.

D] All of the above.

Q.21. . The extensions .gov, .edu, .mil, and .net are called.

A] DNSs.

B] E-mail targets.

C] <u>Domain codes.</u>

D] Mail to address.

Q.22. Web spiders and crawlers are examples of

A] Browsers.

B] <u>Search Engines.</u>

C] HTML Programs.

D] Flames.

Q.23. What is an URL ?

A] A software package used to cruise the World Wide Web..

B] <u>The address of a resource on the World Wide Web.</u>

C] The terms used to describe an internal wizard.

D] A live chat program [Unlimited real time language.

Q.24. What does the abbreviation "www." stands for.

A] <u>World Wide Web.</u>

B] Wide Wide Web.

C] World Width Web.

D] World with Web.

Q.25. Website that allows the user to search for data on keywords is:

A] Chat engines.

B] Routers.

C] Web Server.

D] <u>Search engines.</u>

Q.26. Which of the following web search engine is used worldwide?

A] Domain.

B] <u>Google.</u>

C] Toggle.

D] None of these.

Q.27. When you use a(n) .... to search for a topic, the information you search through is organized into a database like structure.

A] <u>Search engine</u>.

B] Index.

C] Spider.

D] Applet.

Q.28. Which of the following system electronic letter or message sent between individuals or computers.

A] <u>E-mail</u>.

B] Online Service.

C] Share Resources.

D] Voice mail messaging.

Q.29. To add current web to the favourites list.

A] <u>Click "Favourites - Add to Favourites"</u>.

B] Click "Add - Favourites.

C] Click "File - Favourites.

D] All of these.

Q.30. Moving around the web from one site to another is referred to as.................

A] Linking.

B] <u>Navigating</u>.

C] Hopping.

D] Paging.

Q.32. Information sent over the Internet is divided into small pieces called.

A] <u>Packets</u>.

B] PPPs.

C] e-mail forms.

D] Messages.

Q.33. Protocols like PPP and SLIP are used for.

A] <u>Data Transfer</u>.

B] Dialup internet connection.

C] Domain Registration.

D] None of these.

Q.34. The .com indicates websites of.............. Types of organization.

A] <u>Commercial</u>.

B] Complex.

C] Company.

D] Cargo.

Q.35. Sending messages on the internet to another person's mailbox is

A] E-Business.

B] E-Letter.

C] <u>E-Mail.</u>

D] Cyber Mali.

Q.1. This is a type of personal information managers.

A] MS Word 2007

B] MS Excel 2007

C] MS PowerPoint 2007

D] <u>MS Outlook 2007</u>

Q.5. If you want to personalize your work environments wish to use a tool that organizes your contacts. Schedules etc. You will use.

A] Microsoft Office Excel 2007

B] Microsoft Office PowerPoint 2007

C] <u>Microsoft Office Outlook 2007</u>

D] Microsoft Office Word 2007

Q.6. Entry in MS Outlook 2007, that losts for more than 24 hours is called as

A] <u>Event</u>

B] Exhibition

C] Mail

D] Calendar

Q.9. A .... is a descriptive keyboard or phrase used in MS Outlook 2007 in which you can assign related items.

A] <u>Category</u>

B] Mail

C] Notes

D] Point

Q.12. .... are separate external files that are along with you e-mail message.

A] <u>Attachments</u>

B] Options

C] E-mails

D] Parcels

Q.19. You may need to save your contacts to a file, so that are available for use in the future. This is called.................

A] "Saving"

B] "Importing"

C] "Exporting"

D] "Extracting"

Q.28. When you went to convey the information that you have received to your friend or any other person you may .... the mail that you have received.

A] "Share"

B] "Give"

C] "Send"

D] "Forward"

Q.30. The .... is an electronic book, which includes detailed information of all the people with whom you communicate.

A] Address book

B] Calendar

C] Task

D] Notebook

Q.1. When a web site is developed; the various interlinked files are grouped together. This is achieved using which facility.

A] Hypertext.

B] Hyperlinks.

C] Network.

D] None of these.

Q.2. What does the abbreviation "www" in internet stands for:

A] World Wide Web.

B] Wide Wide Web.

C] World Width Web.

D] World with Web.

Q.3. .... is one of the fastest growing internet applications.

A] E-mail.

B] Shopping.

C] Investing.

D] Commerce.

Q.4. .... is the new computer language used to write animation and games for the World Wide Web.

A] Java.

B] C.

C] C++.

D] HTML.

Q.5. .... Include mailing lists news groups and chat groups.

A] <u>Discussion Groups.</u>

B] Internet Groups.

C] IP Groups.

D] All of these.

Q.6. Which of the following is a search engine.

A] Google.

B] Alta Vista.

C] Yahoo.

D] <u>All of these.</u>

Q.8. In IRC, R stands for:

A] Real.

B] <u>Relay.</u>

C] Record.

D] Random.

Q.9. Applets are the special programs written in .... language.

A] <u>Java.</u>

B] HTML.

C] HTTP.

D] None of these.

Q.10. E-mail includes all of the following basic elements except.

A] Header.

B] <u>Footer.</u>

C] Message.

D] Signature.

Q.11. Instant messaging allows you

A] <u>Send E-mail messages.</u>

B] Sharing the data.

C] Instant reply of your messages.

D] To communicate with many at once in a conversation that occurs in real time.

Q.12.] When you use a] n. .... to search for a topic the information you search through is organized into a database - like structure.

A] <u>Search Engine.</u>

B] Index.

C] Spider.

D] Applet.

Q.13. .The extensions .gov, .edu, .mil, and .net are called.

A] DNSs.

B] E-mail targets.

C] <u>Domain codes.</u>

D] Mail to addresses.

Q.14.] Web spider are also known as search engines..

A] True.

B] <u>False.</u>

Q.15.B2c, C2C and B2B are types of...............

A] E-mail.

B] <u>E-commerce.</u>

C] E-cash.

D] All of these.

Q.16. For navigating any website, user has to enter.

A] <u>URL.</u>

B] www.

C] PPP.

D] None of these.

Q.17. Web spiders and Crawlers are examples of

A] Browsers.

B] <u>Search Engines.</u>

C] HTML Programs.

D] Flames.

Q.18. The .com indicates website of .... type of organization.

A] <u>Commerce</u>.

B] Complex.

C] Company.

D] Cargo.

Q.19.ISP stands for.

A] Internal Service Plan.

B] Internet Service Plan.

C] Integral Service Plan.

D] <u>Internet Service Provider.</u>

Q.20............ are programs that provide access to web resources.

A] <u>Browsers.</u>

B] Search Engines.

C] Programs.

D] All of these.

Q.21. Which is a web search engine used World Wide?

A] Domains.

B] <u>Google.</u>

C] Toggle.

D] All of these.

Q.22. Discussion on the internet about specific is known as

A] News.

B] <u>News Group.</u>

C] Veronica.

D] Telnet.

Q.23. Full from of URL

A] Universal Resource Locator.

B] <u>Uniform Resource Locator.</u>

C] Uni Resource Locator.

D] None of these.

Q.24. .... are the special programs written in Java.

A] Java Programs.

B] <u>Applets.</u>

C] Projects.

D] None of these.

Q.25. FTP stands for.

A] Field Transfer Project.

B] File Transfer Project.

C] <u>File Transfer Protocol.</u>

D] None of these.

Q.28. When you type an address such as "http://www.mkcl.org," in this. org indicates that it is a

A] Original Web Site.

B] Commercial Web Site.

C] <u>Organizational Web Site.</u>

D] Educational Web Site.

Q.29. You can seach the World Wide Web for a specific topic by using .... and ....

A] Gophers, Fidos.

B] Scanners, Search engine.

C] <u>Search engine, Index.</u>

D] Browsers, Lukers.

Q.31. A popular chat service is called -

A] Internet Release Chat.

B] Internet Request Chat.

C] Internet Resource Chat.

D] Internet Relay Chat.

Q.33. When you use a] n. .... to search for a topic, the information you search through is organized into a database - like structure.

A] Search Engine.

B] Index.

C] Spider.

D] Applet.

Q.34. The last part of the domain name following the dot .. is called as ....

A] Domain Codes.

B] E-mail Targets.

C] DNSs.

D] Mail to addresses.

Q.35. Following is a script language used, while designing a web page.

A] Hyper Text Mark-up Language.

B] Hyper Link Mark-up Language.

C] Hyper Text Web Language.

D] None of these.

Q.36. What is e-mail?

A] Engineering Mailing.

B] Internet Mailing.

C] Electronic Mailing.

D] All of the above.

Q.37. IM stands for ....

A] Instant Making.

B] Internal Messaging.

C] Instant Messaging.

D] None of these.

Q.39. Directory search is also known as

A] Direct Search.

B] Unique Search.

C] Index Search.

D] All of these.

Q.40. What is URL

A] A software package used to cruise the World Wide Web.

B] The address of resource on the World Wide Web.

C] The term used to describe an internet wizard.

D] Unlimited Real time language.

Q.41. Netscape Navigator is a type of ....

A] Utility Program.

B] Operating System.

C] <u>Browser.</u>

D] Web Authoring Program.

Q.1............ Programs that guard your computer system against viruses or other damaging programs.

A] Backup.

B] <u>Antivirus.</u>

C] Uninstall.

D] None of these.

Q.3. .... is a utility program that locates and eliminates unnecessary fragments and rearranges files and unused disk space to optimize operations.

A] Backup.

B] <u>Disk Defragmenter.</u>

C] Uninstall.

D] All of these.

Q.6............. is the ability of the operating system to run more than one application at a time.

A] Booting.

B] Copping.

C] Pasting.

D] <u>Multitasking.</u>

Q.7............. are used to store data and programs.

A] Folder.

B] <u>File</u>.

C] Recycle bin.

D] None of these.

Q.8. A .... is a connecting ring.

A] <u>Track.</u>

B] Sectors.

C] Round.

D] None of these.

Q.10. Each track is divided into wedge-shaped sections called ....

A] Track.

B] <u>Sectors.</u>

C] Round.

D] None of these.

Q.11............ are also known as service programs.

A] OS.

B] Device Drivers.

C] <u>Utilities.</u>

D] All of these.

Q.12. Type of software that can be described as "end user" software.

A] DOS.

B] System Software.

C] <u>Application Software.</u>

D] Operating Software.

Q.13.GUI Stands for

A] <u>Graphical User Interface.</u>

B] Greater User Interface.

C] Graphical Union Interface.

D] Graphical User Interface.

Q.14. Which of these operating system does not have a graphical user interface ?

A] Windows 95.

B] Mac OS.

C] Linux.

D] <u>MS DOS.</u>

Q.15. Language translators convert the programming instructions, written by programmers into a language that computer understand and process.

A] <u>True.</u>

B] False.

Q.16............ is a collection of several separate troubleshooting utilities.

A] Backup.

B] <u>Norton Utilities.</u>

C] Uninstall.

D] All of the above.

Q.17. .... provides the user interface, controls the computers resources, and runs programs.

A] Drivers.

B] <u>Operating System.</u>

C] Desktop.

D] None of these.

Q.18............ utility identifies non essential files on the hard disk and erases them only when user allows their erasure.

A] Uninstall Program.

B] Backup.

C] File Compression.

D] <u>Disk Clean up</u>.

Q.19. Which of the following is the function of operating system.

A] Managing Resources.

B] Running Applications.

C] Providing User Interface.

D] <u>All of the Above.</u>

Q.20. .... are graphical objects used to represent commonly used applications.

A] GUI.

B] Drivers.

C] Windows NT.

D] <u>Icons.</u>

Q.21. Starting or re-starting a computer is called............. The system.

A] <u>Booting.</u>

B] Copping.

C] Pasting.

D] Multitasking.

Q.22. .... are specialized programs that allow particular input or output devices to communicate with the rest of the computer system.

A] <u>Device Drivers.</u>

B] Utilities.

C] OS.

D] None of these.

Q.24. The .... displays a list of commands that can be used to gain access to information, change hardware settings, find information stored in the, get online help and shut down the computer.

A] GUI.

B] Desktop.

C] Icon.

D] <u>Start Button.</u>

Q.25. Which of the following example of network operating systems ?

A] Netware.

B] Windows N.T. Server.

C] Windows XP Server.

D] All of the above.

Q.27. Which programs reduce the size of the files so that they occupy lesser space on the disk.

A] Backup.

B] Disk Cleanup.

C] File Compression.

D] Uninstall Program.

Q.30. .... convert the programming instruction written by programmers into a language that computers understand and process.

A] Utilities.

B] Device Drivers.

C] Language Translators.

D] None of these.

Q.31. System software includes all of the following except.

A] Operating System.

B] Device Drivers.

C] Utilities.

D] Desktop Publishing.

Q.32. .... is background software that helps the computer manage its own internal resources.

A] System Software.

B] Information.

C] Objects.

D] None of these.

Q.1. Microprocessor has two basic components.

A] Control Unit.

B] Arithmetic Logic Unit.

C] All of these.

D] None of these.

Q.2. Which of the following is a data processing unit

A] CPU.

B] RAM.

C] Hard Disk.

D] Floppy.

Q.5. RISC stands for.

A] <u>Reduced Instruction Set Computer.</u>

B] Read Instruction Set Computer.

C] Reduce Instruction Software Computer.

D] None of these.

Q.6. The........... Connects all system computers and allows input and output device to communicate with the system unit.

A] <u>System Board</u>.

B] Monitor.

C] Mouse.

D] None of these.

Q.7. The types of microprocessor chips are

A] CISC Chips.

B] RISC Chips.

C] <u>All of these.</u>

D] None of these.

Q.9. Which of following is a primary memory ?

A] <u>RAM.</u>

B] CD.

C] Floppy.

D] Hard Disk.

Q.10. Random Access Memory] RAM. is .... type of memory.

A] Permanent.

B] <u>Temporary.</u>

C] Flash.

D] Smart.

Q.14. CISC stands for.

A] Computer Instruction Set Computer.

B] <u>Complex Instruction Set Computer.</u>

C] Complex Index Set Computer.

D] None of these.

Q.16. Note book system units are often called as ....

A] PDA.

B] <u>Laptop.</u>

C] Desktop.

D] None of these.

Q.17. .... is also known as the system cabinet or chassis.

A] <u>System Unit.</u>

B] Monitor.

C] Key board.

D] None of these.

Q.21. Which of the following component is used to store data?

A] CPU.

B] <u>Memory.</u>

C] Input Device.

D] Output Device.

Q.23. In a microprocessor system, the control processing unit] C.P.U.. or processor is contained on a single chip called the ....

A] Slot.

B] Port.

C] <u>Microprocessor.</u>

D] None of these.

Q.24. .... is a 16-bit code designed to support international language like Chinese and Japanese.

A] <u>Unicode.</u>

B] ASSCII

C] EBCDIC

D] None of these.

Q.26. Which of the following is the unit of computer memory.

A] Kilogram.

B] <u>Kilobytes.</u>

A] Meter.

B] Celsius.

Q.29. Which of the following is the highest unit of memory ?

A] <u>Gigabyte.</u>

B] Bytes.

C] Megabytes.

D] Kilobytes.

Q.32. Which of the following is a primary memory?

A] <u>RAM.</u>

B] CD.

C] Floppy.

D] Hard Disk.

Q.4. The keys labelled 0 -9 on the keyboard are called.

A] Function Keys.

B] Typewriters Keys.

C] <u>Numeric Keys.</u>

D] Special purpose Keys.

Q.6. ………. devices translate what people understand into a form that computers can process.

A] Input.

B] Output.

A] <u>All of these.</u>

B] None of these.

Q.7. The keyboards keys that are labelled F1, F2 and so on are called…………….

A] <u>Function Keys.</u>

B] Numeric Keys.

C] Typewriter Keys.

D] Special Purpose Key.

Q.8. Which of the following device is not from pointing type of device?

A] Mouse.

B] Touch screen.

C] <u>Key board.</u>

D] Joystick.

Q.9. which of these is not a input device?

A] <u>Monitor.</u>

B] Mouse.

C] Key board.

D] Joystick.

Q.14. The keyboard keys like caps lock that turn a feature on or off are called.

A] Function Keys.

B] Combination Keys.

C] <u>Toggle Keys</u>.

D] Special Purpose Keys.

Q.17. The mouse pointer seen on the desktop is also called as……………

A] <u>Arrow Pointer.</u>

B] Key Pointer.

C] Display Pointer.

D] None of these.

Q.21. The easiest way to access any part of the screen in the windows operating system is using the

A] Key board.

B] Rat.

C] <u>Mouse.</u>

D] Joystick.

Q.25. Instead of function keys which are use to create a shortcut.

A] Toggle Keys.

B] Special Keys.

C] <u>Combination Keys.</u>

D] Numeric Keys.

Q.28. Which printer print data or image by spraying small drops of ink at high speed into the surface of the paper ?

A] <u>Ink Jet Printer.</u>

B] Laser Printer.

C] Dot Matrix Printer.

D] Drum Printer.

Q.29. Which of the following key is not a toggle key ?

A] Caps Lock.

B] Num Lock.

C] Scroll Lock.

D] <u>Control.</u>

Q.30. The keyboard keys that have arrows on them are called.

A] Function Keys.

B] <u>Navigation Keys.</u>

C] Typewriters Keys.

D] Special Purpose Keys.

Q.31. A .... is a light sensitive pen like device.

A] <u>Light Pen</u>.

B] Joy Stick.

C] Touch Screen.

D] None of these.

Q.33. which of the following device is used to play fast computer games?

A] <u>Joystick.</u>

B] Touch Surface.

C] Touch Screen.

D] Track Ball.

Q.2. Which of these is not a file compressing program ?

A] Win Zip.

B] PK Zip.

C] Win RAR.

D] <u>RAID.</u>

Q.4. .... disk from the Sony Corporation have a capacity of 200 MB or 720 MB.

A] Super Disk.

B] HiFD Disk.

C] Zip Disk.

D] None of these.

Q.6. .... improves hard-disk performance by anticipating data needs.

A] Disk Catching.

B] Disk Defragment.

C] Disk Writing.

D] None of these.

Q.7. 3.5 floppy disk capacity is ....

A] 1.44 MB.

B] 1 MB.

C] 1.66 MB.

D] 1.55 MB.

Q.9. A CD-ROM stands for.

A] Compact Disk Read Only Memory.

B] Compact Disk Read Once Memory.

C] CD-RW.

D] None of these.

Q.10............ Programs that guard your computer system against viruses or other damaging programs.

A] Backup.

B] Anti Virus.

C] Uninstall.

D] None of these.

Q.11. What is the name given to a part of circle on which data is written in a storage media ?

A] Track.

B] Sector.

C] Cylinder.

D] Spiral.

Q.12. A CD-RW Disk means.

A] CD-Rewriteable.

B] CD-Recordable.

C] CD-ROM.

D] None of these.

Q.13. .... are produced by omega and topically have a 100 MB, 250 MB or 750 MB capacity over 500 times as much as today's standard floppy disk.

A] Super Disk.

B] HiFD Disk.

C] <u>Zip Disk.</u>

D] None of these.

Q.16........... are produced by Imation and have a 120 MB or 240 MB capacity.

A] <u>Super Disk.</u>

B] HiFD Disk.

C] Zip Disk.

D] None of these.

Q.17. .... are removable storage devices used to store massive amounts of information.

A] <u>Hard Disk Packs</u>.

B] C.D..

C] Floppy Disk.

D] None of these.

Q.20. The 2 HD on a disk label means.

A] Two side, Low Density.

B] <u>Two Side High Density</u>.

C] One Side High Density.

D] None of these.

Q.21............ disks have a 120 MB storage capacity and the drivers are also able to read and store data on a standard 3.5" floppy disk.

A] <u>Super Disks.</u>

B] HiFD Disks.

C] Zip Disks.

D] None of these.

Q.23. A CD-R stands for.

A] <u>CD-Recordable.</u>

B] CD-Runner.

C] CD-Receiver.

D] None of these.

Q.24. Each track is divided into wedge-shaped sections called.

A] Track.

B] <u>Sectors.</u>

C] Round.

D] None of these.

INDUSTRIAL TRAINING INSTITUTE

Monthly Test-1, Marks- 20, Date:- ________________

(Every Question Carry Two Marks)

7] First aid is given to an injured or ill person primarily....

A] Save life

B] Prevent further deterioration of the muff's

C] Give best possible comfort

D] All of these

84] Which one of the following fire extinguisher is suitable for a live electrical fire?

A] halon

B] water

C] foam

D] liquefied chemical

151] A single wattmeter can be used to measure power in a 3-phase system only when the load is..

A] balanaced

B] unbalanced

C] balanced as well as unbalanced load

D] constant

152] The force producing movement of the pointer in an indicating instrument is called as...

A] deflecting force

B] controlling force

C] damping force

D] distracting force

153] A permanent magnet moving coil instrument will read...

A] only AC quantities

B] only DC quantities

C] both AC and DC quantities

D] pulsating quantities

154] An instrument using gravity control will read correctly if used in..

A] vertical position only

B] horizontal position only

C] inclined position only

D] any position

155] Which one of the following damping methods is used in permanent magnet moving coil instrument?

A] air damping

B] fluid damping

C] spring damping

D] eddy current damping

156] Moving coil instrument works on the effect of...

A] chemical effect

B] heating effect

C] electrostatic effect

D] electromagnetic effect

157] The meter installed at your house to measure electrical energy is an example of...

A] indication type instrument

B] recording type instrument

C] indicating as well as recording type instrument

D] integrating type instrument

158].Which of the following material is preferred for permanent magnet?

A] alnico

B] y-alloy

C] silicon steel

D] wrought iron

INDUSTRIAL TRAINING INSTITUTE

Monthly Test-2, Marks- 20, Date:- ________________

(Every Question Carry Two Marks)

159] The instrument which could be classified as absolute instrument is...

A] milli ammeter

B] micro ammeter

C] galvanometer

D] tangent galvanomer

160] Which of the following methods of damping is commonly used in moving iron instrument?

A] Air damping

B] fluid damping

C] eddy current damping

D] viscosity damping

161] The deflecting torque of a moving iron instrument is directly proportional to the..

A] current

B] square of the current

C] square root of the current

D] voltage

162] Which of the following is used for measuring the medium resistance directly?

A] ammeter

B] megger

C] ohmmeter

D] voltmeter

163] An ohmmeter is used for measuring the...

A] insulation resistance

B] resistance

C] current

D] potential difference

164] Which of the following components is not a part of an ohmmeter?

A] fixed resistor

B] variable resistor

C] capacitor

D] battery

165] In shunt ohmmeter, maximum deflection signifies ..

A] maximum resistance

B] minimum resistance

C] a fault in the megger

D] none of these

166].An unknown DC voltage is to be measured, which measuring range will you select first?

A] 500V

B] 50V

C] 1.5 V

D] 0.5V

167].An unknown direct current of micro ampere rating is to be measured, which measuring range will you select first?

A] 20 micro amp

B] 15 micro amp

C] 150 micro amp

D] 500 micro amp

168] A multimeter cannot measure...

A] current

B] potential difference

C] capacitance

D] resistance

INDUSTRIAL TRAINING INSTITUTE

Monthly Test-3, Marks- 20, Date:- ________________

(Every Question Carry Two Marks)

169] Dynamometer type meters are used to measure...

A] only AC quantities

B] only DC quantities

C] both AC and DC

D] pulsating AC only

170] Which effect is used in wattmeter?

A] electrodynamic effect

B] thermal effect

C] chemical effect

D] electrostatic effect

171] Which of the instrument listed below operates efficiently as wattmeter in both AC and DC?

A] PMMC instrument

B] dynamometer instrument

C] hot wire instrument

D] MI instrument

172] Electrodynamic type of instrument are used commonly for the measurement of...

A] voltage

B] current

C] resistance

D] None of above

173] When the phase and neutral of the energy meter are interchanged, its disc...

A] rotates in reverse direction

B] rotates in correct direction

C] will stop

D] rotates slowly

E] rotates at high speed

174] When the disc of energy meter is rotating even without connecting any load, the error is called

A] creeping error

B] phase error

C] friction error

D] temperature error

175] AC single phase energy meters record the energy in the unit of...

A] kilowatt hours

B] number of thousands of disc rotation

C] volt amperes

D] kilo volt ampere

176] A megger measures resistance in...

A] ohms

B] hundreds of ohms

C] thousands of ohms

D] millions of ohms

177] A megger is exclusively designed for measuring..

A] very high resistance

B] very low resistance

C] ground faults in power lines

D] over loads on DC motors

178] For pipe earthing the minimum internal diameter of galvanized iron of steel pipe required is...

A] 12.5 mm

B] 16mm

C] 3.5 mm

D] 4 m

INDUSTRIAL TRAINING INSTITUTE

Monthly Test-4, Marks- 20, Date:- _______________

(Every Question Carry Two Marks)

179] The earth conductor provides a path to ground for..

A] leakage current

B] over current

C] high voltage

D] circuit current

180] if the size of the circuit copper conductor is 10 sq-mm then the size of earth conductor in G.I] wire should be...

A] 1.5 sq.mm

B] 2.5 sq.mm
C] 5 sq.mm
D] 10 sq.mm
181] One calory is equal to,,,
A] 4187 joules
B] 418.7 joules
C] 41.87 joules
D] 4.187 joules
2. The number of depletion layers in a transistor is ....
A] four
B] three
C] one
D] two
3. The base of a transistor is .... doped
A] heavily
B] moderately
C] lightly
D] none of the above
4. The element that has the biggest size in a transistor is ....
A] collector
B] base
C] emitter
D] collector-base-junction
5. In a pnp transistor, the current carriers are ....
A] acceptor ions
B] donor ions
C] free electrons
D] holes
6. The collector of a transistor is .... doped
A] heavily
B] moderately
C] lightly
D] none of the above
7. A transistor is a .... operated device
A] current
B] voltage
C] both voltage and current
D] none of the above

8. In a npn transistor, ... are the minority carriers

A] free electrons

B] holes

C] donor ions

D] acceptor ions

INDUSTRIAL TRAINING INSTITUTE

Monthly Test-5, Marks- 20, Date:- _______________

(Every Question Carry Two Marks)

9. The emitter of a transistor is .... doped

A] lightly

B] heavily

C] moderately

D] none of the above

10. In a transistor, the base current is about .... of emitter current

A] 25%

B] 20%

C] 35 %

D] 5%

11. At the base-emitter junctions of a transistor, one finds ....

A] a reverse bias

B] a wide depletion layer

C] low resistance

D] none of the above

12. The input impedance of a transistor is ....

A] high

B] low

C] very high

D] almost zero

13. Most of the majority carriers from the emitter ....

A] recombine in the base

B] recombine in the emitter

C] pass through the base region to the collector

D] none of the above

14. The current IB is ....

A] electron current

B] hole current

C] donor ion current

D] acceptor ion current

15. In a transistor ....

A] IC = IE + IB

B] IB = IC + IE

C] IE = IC – IB

D] IE = IC + IB

16. The value of a of a transistor is ....

A] more than 1

B] less than 1

C] 1

D] none of the above

17. IC = aIE + ...

A] IB

B] ICEO

C] ICBO

D] ßIB

18. The output impedance of a transistor is ....

A] high

B] zero

C] low

D] very low

INDUSTRIAL TRAINING INSTITUTE

Monthly Test-6, Marks- 20, Date:- _______________

(Every Question Carry Two Marks)

19. In a tansistor, IC = 100 mA and IE = 100.2 mA. The value of ß is

....

A] 100

B] 50

C] about 1

D] 200

20. In a transistor if ß = 100 and collector current is 10 mA, then IE is

....

A] 100 mA

B] 100.1 mA

C] 110 mA

D] none of the above

21. The relation between ß and a is ....

A] ß = 1 / (1 – a)

B] ß = (1 – a) / a

C] ß = a / (1 – a)

D] ß = a / (1 + a)

22. The value of ß for a transistor is generally ....

A] 1less than 1

B] between 20 and 500

C] above 500

8. At series resonance, the circuit offers .... impedance

A] Zero

B] Maximum

C] Minimum

D] None of the above

9. A resonant circuit contains .... elements

A] R and L only

B] R and C only

C] Only R

D] L and C

10. At series or parallel resonance, the circuit behaves as a .... load

A] Capacitive

B] Resistive

C] Inductive

D] None of the above

11. At series resonance, voltage across L is .... voltage across C

A] Equal to but opposite in phase to

B] Equal to but in phase with

C] Greater than but in phase with

D] Less than but in phase with

12. When either L or C is increased, the resonant frequency of LC circuit ....

A] Remains the same

B] Increases

C] Decreases

D] Insufficient data

13. At parallel resonance, the net reactive component circuit current is ....

A] Capacitive

B] Zero

C] Inductive

D] None of the above

INDUSTRIAL TRAINING INSTITUTE

Monthly Test-7, Marks- 20, Date:- _________________

(Every Question Carry Two Marks)

14. In parallel resonance, the circuit impedance is ....

A] C/LR

B] R/LC

C] CR/L

D] L/CR

15. In a parallel LC circuit, if the input signal frequency is increased above resonant frequency then ....

A] XL increases and XC decreases

B] XL decreases and XC increases

C] Both XL and XC increase

D] Both XL and XC decrease

16. The Q of an LC circuit is given by ....

A] 2pfr x R

B] R / 2pfrL

C] 2pfrL / R

D] R2/2pfrL

17. If Q of an LC circuit increases, then bandwidth ....

A] Increases

B] Decreases

C] Remains the same

D] Insufficient data

Q.14. Which of the following would not be considered as portable computer.

A] Desktop Computer.

B] Note book computer.

C] Personal Digital Assistant.

D] None of these.

Q.19............. is a pointing device.

A] Mouse.

B] Printer.

C] Scanner.

D] Keyboard.

Q.20. The keyboards keys that are labelled F1, F2 and so on are called ....

A] Function Keys.

B] Numeric Keys.

C] Typewriter Keys.

D] Special purpose keys.

Q.21. The keyboard keys like Caps lock that turn on features on or off are called.

A] Function Keys.

B] Combination Keys.

C] Toggle Keys.

D] Special Purpose Keys.

Q.22. Word processing, electronic spread sheets, database managers and graphics programs are all grouped under the title.

A] Browsings Programs.

B] Operating System.

C] Application Software.

D] Data and Information.

Q.23. Keyboard, mouse, monitor, and system unit collectively also known as

A] Solid ware.

B] Software.

C] Hardware.

D] Firm ware.

INDUSTRIAL TRAINING INSTITUTE
Monthly Test-8, Marks- 20, Date:- _______________
(Every Question Carry Two Marks)

Q.29. The keys labelled 0-9 on the keyboard are called.

A] Function Keys.

B] Numeric Keys.

C] Typewriter Keys.

D] Special purpose keys.

Q.31. .... consists of step-by-step introductions that tells the computer how to complete the task.

A] Programs.

B] Hardware.

C] Data.

D] Objects.

Q.33.......... is a background soft ware that helps the computer to manage its internal resources.

A] System Software.

B] Information.

C] Objects.

D] None of these.

Q.35. Following are the file compression programs, EXCEPT

A] Win Zip.

B] RAID.

C] Win RAR.

D] PK Zip.

Q.38. The keyboard keys that have arrows on them are called.

A] Function Keys.

B] Combination Keys.

C] Navigation Keys

D] Special Purpose Keys.

Q.42.......... are graphical objects used to represent and open commonly used applications.

A] G.U.I..

B] Primers'.

C] Windows NT.

D] Icons.

Q.44. Data stored in RAM is

A] Is non-volatile.

B] Is only there while the power is on.

C] Remains only a few minutes after the power is turned off.

D] Is permanent and only lost in power failure.

Q.46. Primary function of a monitor is to display information to the user.

A] True.

B] False.

Q.47. Random Access Memory] RAM. is .... type of memory.

A] Permanent.

B] Temporary.

C] Flash.

D] Smart.

Q.5. You can click on.............. to learn how to use Windows Vista, obtain troubleshooting information, receive support and more.

A] "Search"

B] "Windows"

C] "Start"

D] "Help & Support"

INDUSTRIAL TRAINING INSTITUTE
Monthly Test-9, Marks- 20, Date:- _______________
(Every Question Carry Two Marks)

Q.6. In MS paint to draw a curved line, we have to click the................... Icon.

A] "Curve"

B] "Line"

C] "Polygon"

D] "Rectangle"

Q.7. .... refers to the height and width of the characters to be printed.

A] "Font Size"

B] "Border"

C] "Cell"

D] "Font Style"

Q.8. There is button which is not present on the "Title bar".

A] Minimize

B] Start

C] Maximise

D] Close

Q.9. Disk Defragmenter is used to remove unnecessary files on your hard disk to free up space and your computer run faster.

A] True

B] False

Q.11. To start the calculator application click "Start" and select "All Programs Accessories Calculator."

A] True

B] False

Q.12. .... can be used to create and format large and complex text documents.

A] "Calculator"

B] "WordPad"

C] "Notepad"

D] "Text Pad"

Q.14. A folder system is also called a "..............."

A] "Direction System"

B] "Directory System"

C] "Directory list"

D] "Folder book"

Q.17. A .... is like a container in which you can store files.

A] "Icon"

B] "document"

C] "Folder"

D] "Sheet"

Q.18. The operating system's job is .... to

A] Execute many useful commands easily.

B] to make request for service through a defined application programme interface.

C] to control the computer at the most fundamental level.

D] None of these.

Q.19. The windows interface is based on ....

A] "Graphical user Interface" or GUI

B] Application Programme Interface or] API.

C] "Clipboard"

D] None of these

INDUSTRIAL TRAINING INSTITUTE

Monthly Test-10, Marks- 20, Date:- ________________

(Every Question Carry Two Marks)

Q.51. With the .... option, you can freeze either or both, rows and columns ie. regardless of where you are in the worksheet you can see the information in these rows and/or columns at all times.

A] Split

B] Arrange

C] Fitter

D] <u>Freeze Panes</u>

Q.54. A template file in MS Excel 2007 has an extension "................".

A] .docx

B] .yltx

C] <u>.xltx</u>

D] .zltx

Q.55. A "............" is like an accountant's ledger consisting of rows and columns.

A] Table

B] <u>Microsoft Excel 2007</u>

C] Format

D] Sheet

Q.3. A "................" graphic is a visual representation of your information and ideas.

A] "WordArt"

B] "ClipArt"

C] "SmartArt"

D] "Autoshape"

Q.5. "..............." refer to a ready-to-use picture.

A] "WordArt"

B] "ClipArt"

C] "SmartArt"

D] "Autoshape"

Q.8. The "............." tab contains tools that controls how to slide show is presented.

A] "Design"

B] "Slide Show"

C] "Review"

D] "View"

Q.10. .... which displays icon that represent commonly used commands such as Save, Undo, and Redo.

A] Home Button

B] The Ribbon

C] The Quick Access Tool bar

D] The Office Button

Q.11. A "..........." is a connection to a location in the current documnet, another document or a website.

A] Highlink

B] hipolink

C] linkage

D] hyperlink

Q.12. .... are used to create slide shows on the computer

A] Presentation graphics

B] Analytical development programs

C] Super Slide packages

D] Slide maker tools

Q.15. In graphic presentation, programmes each presentation is divided into ....

A] charts

B] slides

C] tables

D] pictures

INDUSTRIAL TRAINING INSTITUTE

Monthly Test-11, Marks- 20, Date:- _______________

(Every Question Carry Two Marks)

Q.19. A "................" is a pre-designed presentation designed for common purpose such as photo album or a quiz show.

A] "Chart"

B] "Table"

C] "Slide"

D] "Template"

Q.22. When you move your mouse over a sizing handle the pointer becomes a "..............".

A] Round Arrow

B] Two-headed Arrow

C] Plus Sign

D] Four-headed Arrow

Q.23. PowerPoint Presentation is a component of following application software.

A] Leap Office

B] Start Office

C] Open Office

D] MS Office

Q.29. You may change the presentation views by checking on the buttons displayed on the "..........." at the bottom of the screen.

A] "Title bar"

B] "Menu bar"

C] "Tool bar"

D] "Status bar"

Q.33. In Presentation Graphics "..........." are used to add information such as slide numbers, the time and date, a company logo or the presentation title to the top of a handout or notes page in your presentation, or a bottom of a slide, handout or notes.

A] Hyperlinks

B] Tables

C] Header and Footers

D] Charts

Q.35. "................" takes up the full computer screen, like an actual slide show presentation.

A] Slide Sorter View

B] Normal View

C] <u>Slide Show View</u>

D] Notes Page

Q.38. If you have a large number of slides in your presentation, you may find it more convenient to use the .... to view all your slides and change their positions.

A] Normal View

B] <u>Slide Sorter View</u>

C] Slide Show View

D] Notes Page

Q.40. In Microsoft PowerPoint your file is stored with the .... extension.

A] psd

B] .rtf

C] <u>.pptx</u>

D] .docx

Q.41. When the pointer becomes a ...., you can drag placeholder to the location you wish.

A] Round arrow

B] Two-round arrow

C] Plus sign

D] <u>Four-headed arrow</u>

Q.43. "............" are details about a file that help identify it.

A] Desktop Properties

B] Window Properties

C] Advanced Properties

D] <u>Document Properties</u>

INDUSTRIAL TRAINING INSTITUTE

Monthly Test-12, Marks- 20, Date:- _______________

(Every Question Carry Two Marks)

Q.46. "..............." is the main editing view.

A] Slide Sorter View

B] <u>Normal View</u>

C] Slide Show View

D] Notes Page

Q.49. The "............" tab contains the basic formatting tools.

A] "Design"

B] "View"

C] "Insert"

D] "Home"

Q.2. "............." is a database object that is mainly used to enter and display records and make changes to existing records on screens.

A] query.

B] form.

C] report.

D] table.

Q.7. "............." is an electronic database management system which can store, organize access, manipulate, and present information in many different ways.

A] MS Access 2007.

B] MS Word.

C] MS Excel.

D] MS PowerPoint.

Q.11. "............." data type is used to store numbers only.

A] Auto Number.

B] Text.

C] Number.

D] Date/Time.

Q.13. "............" stores the information in Access 2007.

A] Table.

B] Queries.

C] Reports.

D] Forms.

Q.15. "..........." data type is used to store images, documents, graphs etc.

A] Hyperlink.

B] OEL Object.

C] Text.

D] Description.

Q.16. "..........." decides the maximum number of characters that can be entered in the field.

A] Format.

B] Input Mask.

C] Caption.

D] <u>Field Size.</u>

Q.17. The information in a database is stored in a ....

A] Chart.

B] Box.

C] Folder.

D] <u>Table</u>.

Q.18. "............" is the default data type and is used to store text entries like words, combinations of words and numbers and numbers that are not used in calculations.

A] Text.

B] Number.

C] Memo.

D] <u>Currency.</u>